BIBLICAL & PRACTICAL STEPS TO SUCCESS

FOR FIRST RESPONDERS & FAITH-BASED INITIATIVES

Jonathan C. Carey

CAREY PRESS
EQUIPPING ENCOURAGING EMPOWERING

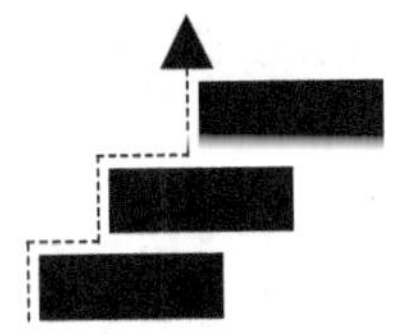

REVIEWS

Our lives are like sand through the hourglass. However, what we do during that passage is what will last, count, and/or add meaning to that period of time.

We cannot and do not see the wind, but we can feel its effect, especially if we observe the windmill. The windmill remains motionless unless the wind is present to drive it into motion. So, too, are humans in the field of protective services, be it first responders, fire, ambulance, police or army, among others. Those who choose to devote their energies to be of service to humanity in these areas of endeavor act as catalysts for change in their local communities. However, it is without doubt that the impact on local communities will certainly transcend to regional and international boundaries.

Dr. Carey's book, *Biblical and Practical Steps to Success,* has skillfully merged the biblical truths and referenced them in a way that illuminates in a profound way how individuals involved in the field as first responders and faith-based organizations aid humanity to make their lives more meaningful.

In a very succinct manner, Dr. Carey's book encapsulates the thoughts of courage, compassion, and compliance, using his real-life experiences, knowledge, and training to give us a blueprint of a road map to success.

It is often said that experience is the greatest teacher. This book brings out Dr. Carey's experience in the field as a first responder while also, in a very scholarly way, linking it to his spirituality and deep faith in God.

I recommend *Steps to Success* to every individual willing to progress toward a fulfilling life of service for their family, friends, community, and the world at large.

The pages of this must-read will certainly grip your attention.

Mr. William J. Harry OBE, JP
Commissioner of Police (Retired)
Saint Vincent and Grenadines

I met Chaplain Jonathan Carey for the first time during our Deployment to Ferguson, Missouri, back in 2014 during times of civil unrest. His courage and compassion were a direct reflection of his personal relationship with the Lord. I look up to and draw from the experience of many men of God; Chaplain Carey is one of those men. In *Biblical & Practical Steps to Success*, Chaplain Carey has expressed what it is to have godly courage, compassion for the grieving, and compliance to the authority of Jesus' leadership. This is another resource that I will be adding to my library.

If you are already serving as a First Responder Chaplain, this book will give you a new and deeper insight in your role. If you are thinking and praying about becoming a First Responder Chaplain, this resource will help you become the best Chaplain you can be.

Thank you, Chaplain Carey, for your godly example and for sharing your real-life chaplain experiences.

Rev. Jason Scalzi
Retired Officer, Vineland, NJ,
Law Enforcement Deployment Manager
Billy Graham Evangelistic Association,
Ordained Chaplain with the Assemblies of God

It is an honor to pen these words for Brother Jonathan Carey's exceptional book, *Biblical and Practical Steps to Success for First Responders and Faith-Based Initiatives*. My connection with Brother Jonathan Carey is divine, leaving an indelible impression on me, particularly through the remarkable commitment to Chaplaincy which he has exhibited in the three years we have known each other.

In 2024, Brother Jonathan and a team of chaplains from the Billy Graham Rapid Response Team visited and held sessions with Zambian Chaplains from the Defence and Security Wings. They also engaged 4,000 church leaders in Kitwe and Lusaka (Zambia) respectively.

This book comes at a crucial juncture, offering invaluable insights and guidance to Chaplains or anyone with a heart to serve and provide spiritual care in times of crisis. Brother Jonathan exemplifies a commitment to service and compassion, qualities that are essential in nurturing the well-being of our communities. This book is a resource that cuts across cultures as it speaks to the Kingdom Principles.

Brigadier General Rev. (Dr.) Henry Matifeyo
Chaplain General, Ministry of Defense
Zambia

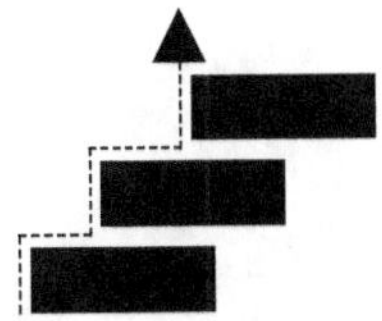

DEDICATION

To the brave men and women of emergency services and community service—the unsung heroes who run towards danger, offering compassion and unwavering teamwork. Your selfless dedication inspires us all, and this book is a humble attempt to honor your service and encourage your hearts.

To my fellow brothers and sisters in Christ, may this work strengthen our resolve to live out our faith in tangible acts of love and service to our neighbors.

And finally, to my family, whose unwavering support and understanding have been my constant rock and foundation throughout the challenges and triumphs of life and ministry. Your love is the greatest gift.

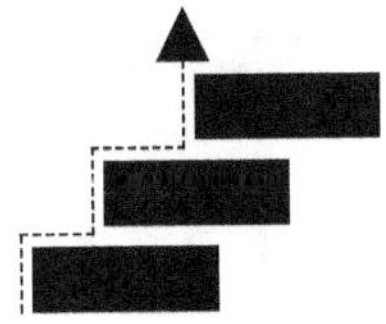

TABLE OF CONTENTS

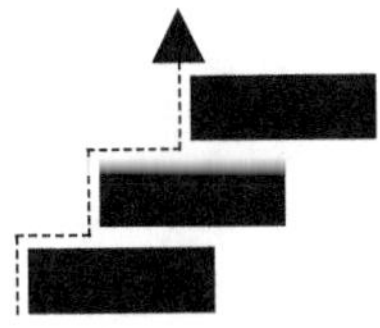

ACKNOWLEDGMENTS

First and foremost, I want to thank my Lord and Savior, Jesus Christ, for the strength, guidance, and unwavering love that have sustained me throughout my life and ministry. This book is a testament to His grace and the transformative power of His love.

My deepest gratitude also goes to my wife, Shena, whose unwavering support, patience, and love have been my constant rock. Her faith and encouragement have been instrumental in the completion of this project. I also extend my heartfelt thanks to my family and friends, whose love and prayers have carried me through the challenges of writing this book.

Finally, I offer my sincere appreciation to all the first responders, community personnel, and volunteers whose tireless dedication inspires me daily. Your selfless service is a true testament to the human spirit, and this book is dedicated to you.

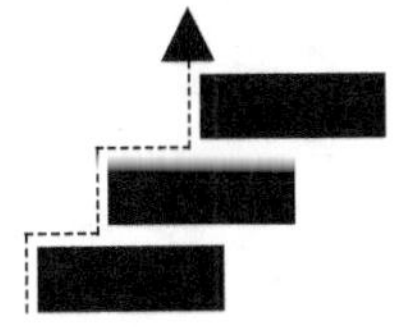

PREFACE

For years, I served navigating the complexities of ministry as a community chaplain and first responder and witnessing firsthand the courage, compassion, and teamwork required to serve. The experiences are etched deeply into my soul, shaping not just my ministry but my very understanding of humanity. The constant pressure, the harrowing realities of human suffering, and the extraordinary acts of selflessness I witnessed sparked a profound reflection: aren't these the same qualities we see reflected in the life and ministry of Jesus Christ?

This book is the culmination of that reflection, a distillation of years spent bridging the seemingly disparate worlds of faith and community service. It's not a mere theological treatise, but a practical guide, intertwining biblical narratives with real-life examples, providing a framework for applying faith to everyday acts of courage, compassion, and teamwork. I pray that this work will not only encourage but also equip you to serve with renewed purpose and unwavering conviction.

Let us, together, heed the call to love our neighbors as ourselves, embodying the very spirit of Christ in our daily lives. This is more than just a book; it's a call to action, a clarion call to be the hands and feet of Jesus in our communities.

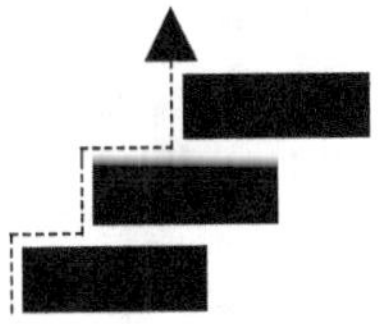

INTRODUCTION

This book takes a unique approach, weaving together the timeless wisdom of scripture with the urgent realities of modern-day service. We will explore the life of Jesus Christ not just as a theological study, but as a living example for those who dedicate their lives to serving others—first responders and every individual striving to make a positive impact. We will delve into the three key characteristics that underpin effective and successful service: courage, compassion, and compliance.

Courage, as exemplified by Jesus' unwavering commitment to truth and justice, even in the face of intense opposition, is a vital ingredient for those who run towards danger, whether it's a burning building, raging storm, or volatile domestic dispute. Compassion, mirrored by Jesus' ministry of presence, His ability to connect with the suffering and marginalized, is the essential ingredient that transforms service from a task to a ministry. Finally, compliance, reflected in the coordinated ministry of Jesus and His disciples, underscores the importance of teamwork and the dangers of self-deployment.

Throughout the book, I will draw upon my experience in community chaplaincy and disaster deployments to illustrate these concepts with real-life examples. These aren't just theoretical ideas; they are principles tested in the crucible of crisis and forged in the fires of human experience. Prepare to be challenged, inspired, and equipped to serve with a renewed sense of purpose. Let the words of this book not be simply read but lived out in your lives—a testament to the transforming power of faith in action.

COURAGE

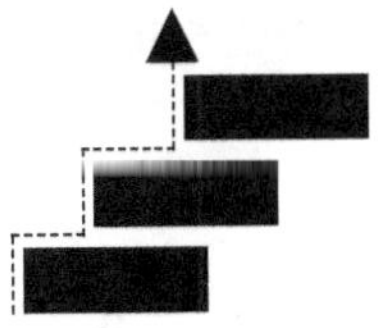

Chapter 1

The Courage of Jesus— A Model for First Responders

The life of Jesus, as depicted in the Gospels, isn't a fairy tale. It's an account of the Son of God serving on earth as the Son of Man who repeatedly chose courage over comfort, love over self-preservation. And this is a powerful lesson for every first responder, for every person who dedicates their life to running towards the fire, towards the chaos and the pain, instead of away from it. We, in our roles, often face situations that mirror, in their intensity and risk, the trials Jesus endured. Think of the cleansing of the Temple. Imagine the scene: the sacred space, profaned, commercialized; the religious leaders, powerful and entrenched, their anger a palpable force. Jesus, unarmed, unaccompanied by a legion of soldiers, walked into that maelstrom. He didn't back down; He didn't hide. He confronted the injustice, the corruption, directly, knowing full well the potential consequences.

His actions weren't reckless; they were brave, fueled by a righteous conviction. They were the embodiment of courage in action, a model we should strive to emulate in our own lives. My own experiences as a first responder have taught me that courage isn't the absence of fear. It's facing down that fear, that primal instinct to run, to protect yourself, and acting despite it.

I remember responding to a domestic disturbance in my community one night. The three-a.m. knock on the front door awakened me to shouts, the shattering of glass, the unmistakable sound of violence escalating. My daughter and I approached our neighbor's home cautiously, hearts pounding, adrenaline surging. We didn't know what to expect; we didn't know the intensity, and we were experiencing a high level of uncertainty. But we went in anyway. We had to. That night, as the adrenaline subsided and the dust settled, the sense of fear remained, but so did a deep sense of satisfaction, knowing that we had done the right thing, that we had acted with courage. And that's precisely what Jesus did. He wasn't immune to fear. He felt the weight of the cross, the agony of betrayal, the sting of rejection. The Garden of Gethsemane, where He prayed so fervently to avoid His fate, is a testament to the very real fear He faced. Yet, He went through with it. He didn't shy away from the suffering, the sacrifice. He chose the path of selfless service, knowing the price. He understood the profound weight of responsibility, the burden of leadership, the inevitable consequences of challenging the established order.

And yet, He persisted. He pressed on, undeterred. This resonates deeply with the experiences of countless first responders who confront the harsh realities of the human condition day in and day out. They step into dangerous situations, they face violent circumstances, they witness unspeakable tragedy. But the similarities extend beyond the dramatic confrontations. Consider Jesus' interactions with the marginalized, the outcasts, the ones society had rejected. He sought them out, listened to their stories, and offered them compassion and healing.

This active engagement with those in desperate need mirrors the work of countless community service personnel who serve on the front lines helping the marginalized, the wounded, those pushed to the edges of society.

This quiet act of reaching out—offering a listening ear, a helping hand—this, too, is an act of courage. It takes courage to approach situations fraught with emotion.

Often you are dealing with people in high-stress, volatile situations. It takes a special type of bravery to maintain composure, to empathize and help, especially when the situation seems intractable. It's courageous to step into the fray, not wielding a weapon but offering comfort.

This isn't to romanticize the profession or ministry. It's brutal, demanding, and emotionally exhausting. The weight of the experiences and the constant exposure to trauma take a toll. It chips away at you, slowly eroding your resilience. We all have seen it firsthand. We watched colleagues, family, and friends struggle with PTSD/PTSI, with burnout, with the profound sense of weariness that comes from bearing witness to so much suffering. It's a heavy burden to carry. The decision-making process under duress—that's a challenge, especially when your choices may have life-altering consequences. It's not only about physical bravery; it's about mental fortitude. This also applies to Jesus' choices—He carefully chose His disciples, prepared them for ministry, and modeled for them resilience through betrayal and suffering.

But within that struggle, within that exhaustion, lies a profound source of strength. And that strength, my friends, is found in the same place Jesus found His: in faith, in community, in the unwavering belief that what we do matters, that our service makes a difference, even in the face of overwhelming odds. It is this same belief that helps first responders and community service personnel navigate their own challenges. It is a belief that allows them to show courage day after day.

This is where faith comes into play. My faith hasn't shielded me from danger; it hasn't erased the fear. But it has given me the courage to face those fears, to run towards the fire, to remain steadfast even when I am exhausted, even when my spirit feels broken. It has provided me with a framework for meaning and purpose within challenges. It's given me a foundation of hope, a source of strength that sustains me through the darkness, through the long nights, through the emotional toll. It's a reminder that even in the face of overwhelming adversity, there is something bigger than us, something stronger than our fear, which guides us, empowers us, helps us to persevere. It allows us to see the light at the end of the tunnel, even when the tunnel seems to stretch endlessly before us. It connects us to a larger community, a larger cause that binds us together and reinforces us. This is particularly crucial in the demanding field of first responding and community services.

Building resilience is not solely about individual strength. It's about fostering strong support networks, about having those to whom we can turn in times of stress, in times of crisis, in times of exhaustion. We can't, and shouldn't, do this alone. Jesus didn't; He had His disciples. He relied on their support, their fellowship, their commitment to His mission. And that is a model of vital importance for all of us, particularly in our lines of work. It's the camaraderie of fellow officers, the bond between firefighters, the mutual respect and support amongst paramedics and crisis personnel; it's the shared burdens and shared joys that make the difference, that keep us going, that bolster our resilience. It is also crucial to acknowledge and address the mental health impacts on first responders and community personnel through proper training, mental health support, and open discussions.

What Jesus didn't model for us He gave to us in examples through parables. One parable to which I will refer often in this book is the parable of the Good Samaritan. The Good Samaritan

didn't walk by; he didn't ignore the suffering. He acted. He showed compassion, risking his own safety and well-being to help someone in need. That is the essence of courageous service. It's the willingness to put ourselves on the line, to go beyond the call of duty, to embrace the challenges, to face our fears, and to serve others, even when it's difficult, even when it's painful, even when it seems hopeless. And it's a reminder that true courage is not found in the absence of fear, but in the triumph over it, in the persistent act of choosing love, of choosing service, of choosing courage, even when it is the hardest path to choose. So let us go forth, emboldened by the example of Jesus, armed with our faith, training, and unwavering commitment to run towards the fire, to be a beacon of hope and a symbol of courageous service in our communities.

Scriptures to Explore

The Cleansing of the Temple: Matthew 21:12–17

The Garden of Gethsemane: Luke 22:40–46

The Good Samaritan: Luke 10:25–37

David and Goliath—
A Biblical Example of Courageous Action

The life of Jesus, a beacon of courage and selfless service, provides an unwavering example for all who dedicate their lives to helping others, especially those in emergency services. But the demonstration of courage isn't limited to the Gospels. The scriptures are replete with accounts of individuals who, against all odds, chose bravery over fear, action over inaction. One of the most compelling and enduring examples is the story of David and Goliath, a narrative that resonates profoundly with the challenges faced by first responders daily.

The valley of Elah, a landscape of tension and dread, served as the stage for a conflict far exceeding the clash of armies. It was a battle between faith and doubt, between hope and despair, between a shepherd boy and a towering giant. Goliath, a Philistine warrior, his armor gleaming menacingly under the harsh sun, stood as a symbol of overwhelming power, a physical manifestation of fear that paralyzed the Israelite army. His very presence instilled terror, a chilling reminder of the seemingly insurmountable odds facing King Saul's forces. Day after day, Goliath's taunts echoed across the valley, a constant barrage of defiance and intimidation intended to break the spirit of the Israelites. Yet, amidst the paralyzing fear, a young shepherd named David emerged. Unlike the seasoned warriors who trembled before Goliath's might, David possessed an unwavering faith, a deep-seated conviction in the power of God. He saw not a monstrous figure of unstoppable power but an adversary to be overcome, a challenge to be embraced.

This wasn't blind faith; it was a faith forged in the crucible of daily life, a faith honed by tending his father's flocks, facing the constant threat of wild animals and harsh weather conditions. His life had prepared him in ways far beyond the rigorous training of the Israelite army.

David's courage wasn't born from a lack of fear. He was acutely aware of the size, strength, and reputation of his opponent. Rather, his courage stemmed from a profound understanding that true strength lies not in physical prowess alone, but in a steadfast belief in God and a resolute commitment to one's faith. This is a crucial distinction, one that often separates the courageous from the merely reckless.

Recklessness is born of impulsivity and a disregard for consequences. Courage, on the other hand, is a conscious choice, a deliberate action fueled by conviction, even in the face of overwhelming odds. David's resourcefulness further underscores his courage. He didn't rely on conventional weaponry or tactics. Instead, he chose the simplest of tools—a sling and five smooth stones. These weren't weapons of war but tools of a shepherd boy, symbols of his humble beginnings. Yet, in his hands, they became instruments of divine intervention, tools of unwavering faith transformed into weapons of incredible power. This highlights the importance of adaptability and innovation, traits that are essential for first responders who constantly encounter unpredictable situations demanding creative solutions. Fire fighters don't rely only on hoses and axes; they must think on their feet, adapt to the unique challenges of each blaze, and often improvise using whatever tools are at hand. The same is true for paramedics facing a critical injury or police and correction officers navigating a volatile situation. Creativity under pressure, like David's resourcefulness, is a form of courage.

The narrative of David's victory isn't about brute force; it's about the triumph of faith over fear, of skill over size, and of courage over intimidation. David's unwavering determination is the most compelling aspect of his story. He did not waver; he did not falter. His commitment was absolute, his belief unshakable. He approached Goliath not with malice, but with unwavering resolve. His focus was not on personal glory, but on delivering his people from oppression.

This unwavering commitment resonates deeply with those in service professions who consistently put themselves at risk for the welfare of others. The firefighter entering a burning building, the police officer confronting a violent suspect, the corrections officer in a confined space, the disaster response volunteer and chaplain in the field, the paramedic rushing to an accident scene—these individuals share David's unwavering commitment to their duty, their dedication to helping those in need, regardless of the personal risk involved.

The parallels between David's actions and those of modern-day first responders are striking. Consider the police officer who confronts an armed suspect: the suspect may be larger, stronger, more heavily armed—a modern-day Goliath. The officer's success doesn't rely solely on physical strength; it depends on training, tactical skills, quick thinking, and, above all, courage—the unwavering determination to protect and serve, even when faced with a threat far exceeding their own physical capabilities. Similarly, the firefighter battling a raging inferno, navigating through smoke and debris, faces immense physical and psychological challenges. The paramedic stabilizing a critically injured patient under chaotic circumstances, facing the emotional weight of life-or-death situations—these are all testaments to a similar type of courage that David exemplified. For those in emergency services, it is a reminder that courage is not the absence of fear, but the ability to overcome it, to act despite the risks, to serve despite the danger. It is a call to embrace our training, to trust in our abilities, and to rely on our faith and unwavering commitment to those we serve.

David's courage was not a singular, isolated act; it reflected his character, which had been shaped by his experiences and strengthened by his faith. This is a testament to the fact that courage isn't merely a quality we possess; it is a virtue we cultivate through consistent action, through the choices we make, and through the challenges we overcome. Furthermore, David's story isn't just a story of individual courage; it's a story about the power of collective action. David's bravery inspired the army, turning their fear into courage, transforming defeat into victory. This collective action is mirrored in the collaborative efforts of emergency response teams. Firefighters, paramedics, correction officers, and police officers often work together seamlessly, coordinating their efforts in a crisis. Their collective courage, the synergy of individual bravery, is what allows them to succeed in situations where individual efforts may fall short. David's victory was a group victory, a testament to the power of faith, unity, and collective action.

The story of David and Goliath resonates deeply with me because it taps into the universal human experience of facing seemingly insurmountable odds. We all encounter situations in our lives where we feel like the underdog, where the challenges seem too great to overcome. The story provides a powerful reminder that with faith, resourcefulness, and unwavering determination, even the most formidable challenges can be conquered. It is a reminder that the battle we face may be large, the adversary imposing, but with God's help, courage can prevail. Like David, we must cultivate our faith, honing our skills and preparing ourselves for the inevitable challenges that lie ahead. The battle may be daunting, but with God's guidance and our unwavering courage, victory will be ours. Let the story of David and Goliath inspire us to run toward the fire, to face our fears, and to serve with courage and unwavering faith. Let it be a constant reminder that true strength lies not in the size of our adversary, but in the conviction of our faith, strength of our spirit, and the unrelenting power of our courage, all empowered by the grace of God.

Scriptures to Explore

1 Samuel 17

The Power of Faith

The Importance of Resourcefulness

The Unwavering Necessity of Courage in the Face of Adversity

Cultivating Courage— Practical Strategies and Techniques

While disembarking the plane in the Republic of Haiti and traveling with the disaster response team to our base camp, the air was thin and contained whispers of anguish, and the rubble of the recent earthquake smelled of decaying flesh. My heart hammered a frantic rhythm against my ribs, a drumbeat echoing the urgency of the situation. But the fear, though present, was no longer paralyzing. It was a fuel, a sharp, insistent reminder of the stakes. Overcoming that initial wave of shock, that primal instinct to second guess my decision to deploy, was the first step, the critical threshold between survival and surrender. And the journey to cultivating that inner strength, that unwavering courage, is a journey of constant practice, of deliberate choices, and of unwavering faith.

For first responders, for those who daily walk the tightrope between life and death, the cultivation of courage isn't a luxury; it's a necessity. It's the difference between a successful intervention and a tragedy, between rescuing a life and losing your own. It's a skill honed not just on the streets or in the field, but within the quiet moments of self-reflection and deliberate preparation. Mental preparedness is paramount. Stress, the insidious enemy of clarity and decisive action, can cripple even the most seasoned professional. Learning to manage stress is not about eliminating it—stress is a natural response to challenging situations. It's about learning to channel it, to transform its destructive potential into focused energy. Techniques like deep breathing exercises, progressive muscle relaxation, and mindfulness meditation can be invaluable tools. These aren't esoteric practices; they're practical, readily accessible methods proven to calm the nervous system and sharpen mental acuity.

Picture this: you are facing a volatile situation, adrenaline surging, heart pounding. Taking slow, deep breaths, focusing on the rhythm of your inhales and exhales, can be the anchor that keeps you grounded, preventing you from being swept away by the chaotic current of fear.

Mindfulness, the practice of paying attention to the present moment without judgment, is equally crucial. It allows you to detach from the swirling anxieties of the future and the regrets of the past, focusing instead on the immediate task at hand. This present-moment awareness can be the difference between a reactive, impulsive response and a calm, calculated action. Regular practice, even just a few minutes a day, can cultivate a mental resilience that allows you to navigate the most challenging situations with greater composure and clarity. I have found only two days that rob me of the focus of today. They are yesterday and tomorrow. Imagine yourself in a high-pressure situation, able to observe your own reactions without getting overwhelmed by them. This conscious awareness allows you to make better decisions, to act with more precision and less fear. This is embracing the experience of today.

Physical preparedness is equally important. Maintaining peak physical condition is not just about looking good; it's about having the stamina and strength to endure physically demanding situations. Regular exercise, a balanced diet, and sufficient sleep are non-negotiable. The body is the instrument of courage, and it needs to be finely tuned and well-maintained. Consider the firefighter, carrying heavy equipment up a burning staircase, the disaster response volunteer removing heavy debris, the corrections officer on the night shift in a room with the incarcerated, or the police officer sprinting after a fleeing suspect. Physical fitness isn't just about strength; it's about endurance, agility, and the ability to perform under pressure. A strong body translates to a stronger mind, boosting confidence and reducing the feeling of vulnerability.

Beyond individual preparation, the strength of a team is an indispensable factor. Building strong, supportive relationships with colleagues is crucial. Trust, mutual respect, and a shared understanding of your roles and responsibilities are essential for effective teamwork. Team-building activities, regular training exercises, and open communication channels all foster a sense of camaraderie and mutual support. Knowing that you can rely on your team, that they have your back, is a powerful antidote to fear.

This is more than just a professional relationship; it's a brotherhood, a sisterhood forged in shared experience and mutual reliance. Imagine a scenario where a colleague is injured. The bonds of a well-trained, supportive team ensure a swift, efficient response, reducing the likelihood of further harm.

Faith plays a pivotal role in bolstering courage. For many, faith provides a source of unwavering hope and resilience, a belief that even in the darkest moments, there is a guiding hand, a God that offers strength and comfort. This faith isn't just about abstract theological concepts; it's a tangible source of strength in times of crisis. It's about connecting with God who is larger than oneself, finding solace in a belief system that provides meaning and purpose. It's about remembering that even in the face of adversity, there is hope, a promise of redemption and renewal. This spiritual grounding can be incredibly powerful, offering a sense of peace and unwavering resolve in the face of fear.

Self-belief is another crucial component. Knowing your capabilities, understanding your training, and having confidence in your abilities is essential for acting decisively and effectively. This isn't about arrogance; it's about recognizing your own strengths and having the self-assurance to trust your instincts. Regular self-assessment, honest reflection on past experiences, and continuous learning are all vital for building this self-confidence. Imagine yourself facing a difficult situation. Self-belief provides the inner strength to confront the challenge, knowing that you possess the skills and the resilience to overcome it.

Finally, the unwavering support of a strong support network is indispensable. This network extends beyond your colleagues; it encompasses family, friends, mentors, and community members who provide emotional sustenance and unwavering encouragement. Sharing your experiences, both triumphs and failures, with trusted individuals allows you to process emotions, gain valuable perspectives, and receive the emotional support you need to navigate the challenges of your profession. No one should act as an island unto themselves. These relationships provide a safe space to reflect, decompress, and recharge, ensuring that you're equipped to face future challenges with renewed strength and resolve. Knowing that you have a network of caring individuals who understand your struggles and celebrate your successes can be profoundly empowering, strengthening your resolve and fueling your courage.

The path to cultivating courage is not a single, linear progression; it's a continuous process of learning, adapting, and growing. It's a journey that requires consistent self-reflection, deliberate practice, and an unwavering commitment to self-improvement. It involves mastering mental and physical disciplines, building strong relationships, cultivating faith, and nurturing a deep sense of self-belief. But the rewards are immeasurable—the ability to face fear head-on, to run towards the fire, not away from it, and to emerge from the most challenging situations stronger, more resilient, and deeply fulfilled. True courage is not the absence of fear, but the triumph over it, fueled by faith, grounded in training, and fortified by the love and support of those around us.

The concept of running towards the fire instead of away from it isn't just about physical bravery; it's about spiritual courage as well. It's about confronting our own fears, biases, and weaknesses, and striving to become better versions of ourselves. It's about embracing the challenges of life, not as insurmountable obstacles but as opportunities for growth and transformation. This spiritual courage is fueled by a deep sense of purpose and a belief in God who is larger than us—a belief that gives us strength when we feel weak, hope when we feel despair, and the conviction that we can make a difference in the world.

My faith doesn't provide a shortcut to avoiding difficult situations or magically eliminating hardship. Instead, it equips me with the inner resilience to face challenges head-on. It instills within me a sense of purpose, a belief that even amid chaos and uncertainty, a divine plan is unfolding. It's the unwavering conviction that, through faith, I can find strength in my weaknesses, hope in despair, and purpose in service.

Spiritual growth is an ongoing process, a journey of constant self-reflection, prayer, and intentional engagement with my faith. It's not simply a matter of attending church services or reciting prayers; it's a deeper commitment to aligning my thoughts, words, and actions with my values and beliefs. This means engaging in consistent self-reflection, evaluating my actions and attitudes, and striving to live in accordance with my faith. It involves actively seeking opportunities to serve others, to extend compassion, and to share my faith in a meaningful and impactful way.

The cultivation of faith isn't a passive pursuit; it demands active engagement. It requires investing time in prayer, studying scripture, and participating in community worship. These practices nurture spiritual growth and deepen our connection with God, providing strength and guidance in our daily lives. The act of prayer, for example, is not simply asking for something; it's a communion with God, a chance to align our will with His and to receive comfort, strength, and guidance. The study of scripture provides wisdom and understanding, offering insights into life's challenges and the paths towards overcoming them (Proverbs 3:5-6). Community worship fosters fellowship, mutual support, and a sense of belonging.

The rewards of cultivating a strong faith are immeasurable. It brings a sense of peace and tranquility that transcends the anxieties and stresses of daily life. It promotes resilience in the face of adversity, allowing us to navigate challenges with greater strength and grace. It provides hope and purpose, giving us the courage to confront our fears and pursue our dreams.

In conclusion, my faith has been a cornerstone of my journey as a first responder and community chaplain. It's not a separate element, but an integral part of who I am and how I approach life's challenges. It's the unwavering foundation upon which I have built my courage, resilience, and unwavering commitment to serving others. Faith provided a strength that enabled me to run towards the fire and emerge stronger on the other side. Even in the darkest of nights, the light of faith can illuminate our path.

COMPASSION

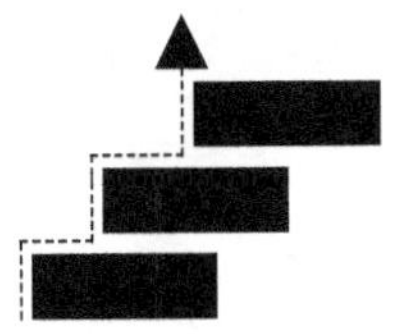

Jesus' Compassion— A Model for Empathy and Understanding

Jesus, Heaven's sent Savior and Earth's Itinerant Preacher, wasn't just a miracle worker; He was a master of presence, a virtuoso of compassion. His ministry wasn't confined to grand pronouncements from mountaintops; it was woven into the fabric of everyday life, a tapestry of encounters with the broken, the marginalized, and the forgotten. To understand Jesus' compassion is to grasp the very essence of His ministry, a ministry that continues to resonate with profound impact in our own lives, especially within the demanding context of first response and community service.

Consider the woman caught in adultery, a woman condemned by the rigid legalism of her time, a woman ostracized and ready to be stoned. The Scribes and Pharisees, eager to entrap Jesus, presented her as a living embodiment of their self-righteous judgment. They anticipated a condemnation, a reinforcement of their own harsh doctrines. Instead, Jesus offered something utterly transformative: a radical act of compassion. He didn't condemn her; He didn't condone her actions; He simply offered a profound and transformative question: "Let he who is without sin cast the first stone" (John 8:7).

This wasn't merely a legal loophole, a clever escape from a difficult situation. It was a profound act of empathy, a recognition of the woman's humanity beyond her transgression. It was an acknowledgment that judgment, without compassion, is inherently flawed, failing to account for the complex tapestry of human experience, sin, and forgiveness. Jesus didn't ignore the societal norms; He subverted them with an act of grace, turning the gaze of judgment inward and offering the woman a pathway to redemption. This wasn't a passive compassion; it was an active intervention, a ministry of presence that moved beyond condemnation to offer restoration.

His interactions extend beyond this single example. His healing ministry, consistently portrayed in the Gospels, is not solely about physical restoration; it's a profound illustration of His compassionate engagement with suffering. Jesus didn't merely heal the sick; He touched the lepers, the outcasts, those society deemed unclean and unworthy. He entered their world, offering not just physical healing but also emotional and spiritual restoration. He saw beyond the symptoms of disease, recognizing the pain, the isolation, and the despair. He didn't just heal their bodies; He healed their souls. This holistic approach underscores the profound depth of His compassion, a compassion that transcends physical limitations to embrace the whole person.

This ministry of presence, this deep-rooted empathy, provides a powerful model for first responders and community service personnel. Imagine a chaplain and police officer arriving at a home to give a death notification, or at the scene of a domestic dispute, not only focusing on the immediate safety of the situation but also recognizing the underlying emotional trauma, fear, and desperation. Imagine them listening with empathy, offering a

calm and reassuring presence, acting as a stabilizing force in a chaotic environment. This isn't simply about enforcing the law; it's about extending compassion, providing a lifeline in a moment of profound crisis. This requires more than just technical skill; it requires emotional intelligence, the capacity for empathy, and the ability to connect with another human being on a deeply personal level.

Similarly, consider a paramedic responding to a medical emergency. The focus, of course, is on providing the best possible medical care. But true compassion extends beyond medical proficiency. It includes acknowledging the fear of the patient and their family, offering comfort and reassurance in a time of vulnerability. It is about the ministry of presence—being there, not just as a medical professional but as a human being who cares. The compassion of Jesus lies in the ability to connect to those He encounters, showing that they are seen, heard, and valued.

This is a challenge, particularly in professions characterized by high-stress environments and emotional exhaustion. First responders and community service personnel often face situations that are deeply unsettling, emotionally draining, and potentially traumatizing. The continuous exposure to human suffering can lead to compassion fatigue, a state of emotional depletion that diminishes the capacity for empathy and effective service. This is where the example of Jesus becomes even more crucial. His ministry wasn't without its difficulties; He faced opposition, rejection, and ultimately, crucifixion. Yet, His compassion never wavered. The key, then, is not only to replicate Jesus' miraculous healings, but also emulate His unwavering commitment to the marginalized. It is about cultivating a spirit of empathy, a deep understanding of the human condition, and the unwavering commitment to meeting people where they are.

This means developing emotional intelligence, understanding the importance of active listening, and learning to discern the underlying emotional needs of the individuals we serve. It is about recognizing that our service extends beyond the immediate task; it is a ministry of presence, an act of grace, a tangible expression of God's love.

Furthermore, Jesus' ministry wasn't performed in isolation. He built a team, choosing disciples to work alongside Him. This collaborative spirit is another vital lesson for first responders and community service personnel. Effective teamwork is essential for efficient and effective service, especially in high-pressure situations. First responders acting alone, without the support and collaboration of their team, risk jeopardizing their safety and the well-being of those they are attempting to help. Likewise, in community service, collective action amplifies the impact of individual contributions, generating a much broader positive ripple effect.

Jesus' ministry serves as a profound reminder that true service isn't simply about performing a task; it's about engaging with people in a compassionate and holistic manner. It's about recognizing the sacred worth of every human being, regardless of their background or circumstances. It's about embracing the ministry of presence, offering empathy, and providing support in times of need. By drawing inspiration from Jesus' life and ministry, first responders and community service personnel can enhance their effectiveness, cultivate resilience, and ultimately transform the lives of those they serve as well as their own.

The path toward greater effectiveness in service is paved with the principles of courage, compassion, and compliance, with the model of Jesus Christ providing a beacon to guide us forward. His ministry isn't just history; it's a living example, a timeless call to action that inspires and challenges us to be better in our service of others. The relentless pursuit of empathy and the active demonstration of compassion in the face of adversity and personal exhaustion define the enduring legacy of Jesus' ministry of presence, providing an unwavering example for all who dedicate their lives to serving others.

The Importance of Active Listening in Crisis Response

The heart of compassionate service, as exemplified by Jesus, isn't merely in the actions taken but in the profound connection forged with those in need. This connection is built upon a cornerstone of effective crisis response: active listening. It's a skill honed not just through training manuals, but through a genuine desire to understand, to empathize, and to see the individual beyond their immediate crisis. It's about hearing the unspoken words, the silences that often speak volumes, and the subtle cues that betray underlying emotions and concerns.

Think again of the parable of the Good Samaritan; it wasn't merely the physical aid offered that defined the act of compassion, but the Samaritan's willingness to stop, to listen, and to truly engage with the suffering man. This active listening isn't passive hearing; it's a conscious, deliberate act of engaging with another human being at their most vulnerable time.

In emergency response situations, active listening is paramount. A police officer encountering a distraught victim of a crime, for instance, cannot simply rush into collecting facts and statements. The officer must first create a safe space, a haven of calm amidst the storm of emotions. This involves more than just a reassuring tone; it requires actively listening to the victim's narrative, allowing them to express their fear, their anger, their grief without interruption or judgment. The officer's body language must reflect empathy—open posture and attentive gaze while minimizing distractions.

These seemingly small actions create a foundation of trust, essential for gathering accurate information and providing effective support. Imagine a situation where a victim of domestic abuse is hesitant to disclose the full extent of the abuse. An officer who rushes the interview, failing to create that space of trust and understanding, risks missing crucial details that could endanger the victim or hinder the investigation. By actively listening, demonstrating genuine care, and patiently allowing the victim to share their story at their own pace, the officer fosters a relationship of trust that can lead to a successful outcome. Furthermore, active listening in such situations can offer emotional validation to the victim, providing a vital lifeline during a time of intense trauma.

The application of active listening transcends the realm of law enforcement and extends into all areas of community service. A social worker interacting with a family facing eviction, for example, needs to go beyond merely assessing their immediate needs. Active listening allows the social worker to uncover the root causes of the crisis, the underlying stressors that may have contributed to their situation. It's about understanding their fears, their anxieties, their hopes for the future. It's about hearing the story behind the numbers, the struggles hidden behind the statistics. Perhaps the family is facing job loss, medical debt, or relationship issues. By carefully listening, social workers gain a deeper understanding of the family's circumstances, enabling them to tailor their assistance to specific needs. This might involve connecting people with job training programs, medical assistance, or marital counseling, rather than simply providing a temporary housing solution. The key here is to avoid solutions imposed from the outside; true compassion lies in listening first, understanding, and then working collaboratively with the family to find a path forward.

Active listening is not merely about hearing the words spoken; it is about understanding the unspoken emotions, the subtext that accompanies every utterance. It requires a keen awareness of nonverbal cues: body language, facial expressions, tone of voice. A slumped posture, averted gaze, or trembling voice may signal underlying distress or anxiety that goes unsaid. A social worker might notice a child exhibiting unusual behavior during a family interview, prompting further investigation into potential abuse or neglect. A police officer might observe a suspect's fidgeting and nervous demeanor, prompting them to probe further into their involvement in a crime. These subtleties frequently offer crucial insights that contribute to a more comprehensive understanding of the situation. Therefore, active listening entails more than just concentrating on the verbal communication; it involves being fully present, observing the whole person, and allowing intuition to guide the interaction.

Furthermore, active listening requires patience, a virtue often in short supply in crisis situations. Individuals facing trauma or distress may struggle to articulate their thoughts and feelings clearly. They may ramble, repeat themselves, or become emotionally overwhelmed. Active listening demands the patience to allow these individuals to process their experiences at their own pace, without interruption or judgment. Interrupting or impatiently redirecting the conversation can undermine the trust and rapport that is crucial for effective intervention. The process needs to be allowed to unfold organically, creating a safe and supportive space for the expression of difficult emotions. This patient attentiveness allows for a deeper connection, revealing aspects of the situation that might otherwise remain hidden.

An essential component of active listening is maintaining a non-judgmental attitude. This doesn't mean condoning harmful behavior, but rather approaching the situation with empathy and understanding. Judging individuals based on their circumstances or choices will inevitably create barriers to communication. It is crucial to approach each interaction with a genuine desire to understand the individual's perspective, even if their actions are questionable. By removing judgment, we foster a climate of trust and safety, allowing individuals to share their experiences openly and honestly, without fear of condemnation. For example, in a case involving substance abuse, an officer who approaches the individual with judgment and disdain is far less likely to gain cooperation or elicit helpful information than an officer who demonstrates empathy and understanding. This approach is crucial not only for gathering information, but also for fostering a positive therapeutic relationship that can motivate the individual towards rehabilitation.

Finally, genuine care is the bedrock of effective active listening. It's about being truly present, emotionally invested in the well-being of the person with whom you are interacting. It's about showing that you care, not just through words but through actions. The simple act of offering a glass of water or a comforting touch can communicate a level of genuine concern that words alone cannot convey. This caring approach transcends the mere exchange of information; it is about building a human connection, recognizing the inherent dignity and worth of every individual, regardless of their situation. This is not just about providing a service; it is about engaging in a shared human experience, recognizing the profound impact of empathy and genuine connection on those in crisis. In essence, it is about embodying the very spirit of the Good Samaritan, offering not just aid, but a presence that offers

hope and healing. The ministry of presence, in this context, is a ministry of attentive listening, a powerful tool that can transform crises into opportunities for healing and growth.

Developing Compassion— Personal Reflection and Exercises

The quiet strength of the paramedic holding a dying man's hand, the unwavering patience of the social worker navigating a family's crisis, the compassionate ear of the chaplain listening to a victim's trauma—all underscore a crucial truth: empathy isn't a passive trait; it's a muscle that strengthens with intentional exercise. It's a spiritual discipline, a way of being, that requires cultivation and practice. Just as first responders hone their skills through rigorous training, we too must actively nurture our capacity for compassion. This section is dedicated to that very process—a journey of self-discovery and intentional practice designed to deepen our empathetic responses and strengthen our ability to minister through presence.

The first step towards developing compassion lies in self-awareness. We can't genuinely connect with others' suffering if we haven't first examined our own emotional landscape. This isn't about self-indulgence; it's about gaining a clearer understanding of our biases, prejudices, and emotional activators. Only through honest self-reflection can we begin to dismantle the walls that prevent us from truly seeing and understanding others.

Take a moment right now, close your eyes, and breathe deeply. Ask yourself: What are my earliest memories of experiencing compassion? Who were the individuals who showed you compassion, and how did their actions affect you? Consider both positive and negative experiences—times when you felt deeply understood and times when you felt misunderstood or dismissed.

What emotions did these experiences evoke? By excavating these memories, we begin to unearth the foundation of our understanding of compassion and identify the patterns that shape our responses to others.

Journaling can be a powerful tool in this process. Take some time each day—even just five or ten minutes—to record your reflections. Describe situations where you felt compassion and analyze what prompted that feeling. Consider situations where you struggled to feel compassion and explore the reasons behind that difficulty. Don't shy away from difficult emotions; allow yourself to feel them fully, acknowledging their presence without judgment. The act of writing down these thoughts allows for a level of self-examination that's often impossible through introspection alone.

Next, let's consider the role of emotional intelligence in cultivating compassion. Emotional intelligence involves the ability to understand and manage our own emotions and to empathize with and understand the emotions of others. It's about recognizing the subtle cues in body language, tone of voice, and facial expressions that can tell us much about a person's inner world. It's about being able to separate a person's actions from their inherent worth. A storm victim's actions are not a defining measure of their humanity, much in the same way a person struggling with addiction retains their inherent dignity. We are called to empathize with their struggles and their humanity, while also acting to safeguard the well-being of the community.

To enhance your emotional intelligence, try this exercise: Observe people in different settings—on public transportation, in a coffee shop, at a community event. I often practice this exercise at airports enroute to a speaking engagement or deployment. Focus on noticing their non-verbal cues. What are their expressions

communicating? What can you infer about their emotional state? Try to construct a narrative about their possible experiences based on those observations. Remind yourself that you see only a small fragment of their reality, and refrain from making judgments. The goal here is to practice observation and interpretation, sharpening your ability to perceive and understand the emotions of others.

Let's delve into the practical application of compassion. Consider participating in a volunteer activity that places you in direct contact with individuals facing challenges. This could range from serving meals at a homeless shelter to assisting at a local animal rescue. The experience of directly witnessing human suffering and offering assistance can be profoundly transformative. It provides opportunities to hone your empathetic skills in tangible ways, building your capacity to respond effectively and compassionately to individuals in need.

The act of service is often more impactful than mere financial contributions. It fosters true connection and strengthens community bonds. But even without formal volunteer work, you can incorporate practices to cultivate compassion into your daily life. Practice active listening—truly hearing and understanding what others are saying, without interrupting or formulating your response. Put down your phone; look them in the eye and make eye contact. Give your complete attention to their words. The act of listening becomes an act of care. Ask open-ended questions that encourage them to share their thoughts and feelings. Show genuine interest in their lives, even if their experiences differ greatly from your own.

Role-playing can also be a valuable tool. Imagine scenarios where you might encounter someone in distress—a distraught parent, a grieving friend, a lost child. Practice responding with compassion, emphasizing active listening, and validating their feelings. You can even do this exercise with a friend, taking turns role-playing different situations. This allows for experimentation and constructive feedback, providing safe space for improving your communication skills and compassionate presence. Moreover, cultivate self-compassion. Compassion is not solely for others; it's equally crucial for us. We must treat ourselves with the same kindness and understanding we extend to others. Acknowledge your own struggles and imperfections without harsh self-criticism. Recognize that setbacks and failures are inevitable parts of life and learn from them rather than letting them define you. Practicing self-compassion allows us to be more resilient and better equipped to offer compassion to those around us. It is a continuous journey, and not a destination.

Finally, remember that developing compassion is a lifelong journey, not a destination. It's a process of continuous learning and growth. There will be times when you fall short; times when you struggle to extend compassion, even to those who deserve it most. This is not a failure, but an opportunity for reflection and further learning. Be patient with yourself; celebrate your progress and acknowledge your imperfections. The path to becoming a more compassionate individual is filled with challenges and victories.

The rewards, however, are immeasurable. Through intentional practice and genuine commitment, we can transform ourselves and build a more compassionate world, one interaction at a time. The ability to empathize with others and to offer them a listening ear, a shoulder to lean on, or simply a kind word, is a gift of immeasurable value—a gift that can change the course of an individual's life and help to heal the world.

This ministry of presence is not merely a concept; it's a powerful tool for transformation that begins within us. By cultivating compassion, we not only improve the lives of others,

but we enrich our own in ways that transcend our wildest expectations. The path to cultivating compassion is a journey of continuous growth, a lifelong process of self-reflection, active listening, and genuine engagement with the needs of those around us. Embrace the journey and allow it to transform both you and those you serve.

Compassion and Spiritual Growth— A Deeper Look

The previous section emphasized the practical application of compassion. But compassion, in its truest form, transcends mere human effort. It finds its deepest roots in the spiritual realm, drawing sustenance from a wellspring of faith and love that empowers us to reach beyond our limitations. This is where the transformative power of compassion truly unfolds.

Think one more time of the parable of the Good Samaritan. It wasn't just a matter of practical aid; it was an act of radical empathy fueled by a profound recognition of shared humanity. The Samaritan, a member of a despised group, disregarded societal norms and religious prejudice to offer selfless compassion to a stranger in desperate need. His actions weren't simply a display of good Samaritanism—they were a testament to the transformative power of a love that breaks down walls and transcends boundaries. This love isn't merely an emotion; it's a spiritual force, a divine strength that compels us to act with kindness and understanding, even towards those we might otherwise reject.

This spiritual dimension of compassion isn't limited to religious individuals. Even those who don't identify with organized religion can tap into this wellspring of empathy through practices that foster self-awareness and connection to something larger than themselves. Consider the profound sense of peace and interconnectedness that comes from spending time in nature, meditating, or engaging in acts of service. These experiences often activate a shift in perspective, fostering a greater appreciation for the fragility and beauty of life. This heightened awareness naturally expands our capacity for empathy and compassionate action. I believe, for many, this is the beginning of recognizing that the heavens declare the glory of God (Psalm 19:1) and becomes one instrument of introduction into His presence. Another instrument is love, one of God's characteristics (1 John 4:16).

The connection between spiritual practice and emotional intelligence is undeniable. Spiritual disciplines, such as prayer, meditation, and mindfulness, cultivate self-awareness—a crucial component of emotional intelligence. When we take the time to quiet our minds and connect with our inner selves, we become more attuned to our own emotions and those of others. This enhanced emotional sensitivity allows us to better understand and respond to the needs of those around us, creating space for authentic empathy and compassionate action.

For example, consider the practice of contemplative prayer. It's not simply about reciting words; it's about creating a space for quiet reflection, allowing God's love to permeate our hearts. This quiet contemplation allows us to connect with a source of unconditional love and acceptance, expanding our capacity for empathy and compassion. It helps us to understand not only our own suffering, but also the suffering of others. This understanding then motivates us to act, to offer comfort and support, even when it's challenging.

The practice of mindfulness similarly fosters emotional intelligence and compassion. By paying attention to the present moment, without judgment, we become more aware of our own thoughts and feelings, and those of others. This awareness

allows us to respond to situations with greater clarity and understanding. Instead of reacting impulsively, we can choose to act from a place of empathy and compassion. Moreover, regular engagement in spiritual practices—be it prayer, meditation, or simply spending time in quiet reflection—cultivates a sense of humility. Humility recognizes our limitations and our shared humanity. This understanding helps us to approach others with compassion, recognizing that everyone carries their own burdens and struggles. It helps to temper our judgment and fosters a sense of understanding and acceptance.

The impact of spiritual growth on compassionate service is profound and far-reaching. It's not just about helping individuals in immediate need. It's about cultivating a fundamental shift in perspective, seeing ourselves as interconnected members of a larger community. This expanded sense of connection fuels a desire to contribute to the well-being of others, not just out of a sense of obligation, but out of genuine love and concern. It's a change of heart that motivates us to actively work for safer communities, environmental protection, and other causes that benefit humanity as a whole.

Think of Mother Teresa. Her life was a powerful testament to the transformative power of faith-inspired compassion. Her tireless work with the poor and marginalized wasn't just driven by a sense of duty; it was fueled by a deep and abiding faith that saw Christ in every individual she served.

This spiritual understanding guided her actions, providing her with the strength and perseverance to continue her work despite unimaginable challenges. Similarly, the work of countless others—from social workers to healthcare professionals to community volunteers—is often motivated by a deep sense of spiritual purpose. Their commitment stems from a belief in the inherent worth of every human being and a desire to create a more just and compassionate world. This isn't simply altruism; it's a manifestation of their spiritual beliefs in action.

However, the path to cultivating compassion, especially when viewed through a spiritual lens, is not always easy. It requires consistent self-reflection, a willingness to confront our own biases and prejudices, and a commitment to personal growth. This process can be challenging, requiring us to examine our own emotional responses and confront the uncomfortable truths about ourselves and the world around us. We might encounter setbacks and moments of doubt, testing our resolve and our commitment to living a compassionate life. But these challenges should not deter us from pursuing this path. The rewards are immeasurable, both for us and for those we serve. The journey of cultivating compassion is a lifelong process of growth and transformation. It is a journey that requires courage, perseverance, and a deep commitment to living a life of faith and love. It is a journey that leads not only to personal enrichment but also to a more compassionate and just world.

Through intentional spiritual practices, we can cultivate a deeper sense of empathy and understanding, allowing us to connect with others on a profound level. This connection is the foundation for true compassion. It empowers us to respond to suffering with kindness, patience, and genuine care. It's not a passive act, but a dynamic process that requires constant nurturing and refinement.

It requires us to be actively engaged with our communities, listening to the stories of others, and responding with empathy and understanding. It's about recognizing our shared humanity and acting accordingly. It's about acknowledging the inherent dignity of every individual, regardless of their background or

circumstances. It involves challenging our own preconceived notions and biases, striving to see the world through the eyes of others. I once heard we are to treat others not how we want to be treated, but rather how they wish to be treated. This was enlightening for me, and it has become my golden rule.

The journey toward cultivating compassion, therefore, is both a personal and spiritual one. It requires self-awareness, humility, and a commitment to personal growth. It is a journey that will transform not only our relationship with others, but also our relationship with ourselves and with God. It's a journey worth taking, one that will lead to immeasurable rewards, both personally and for the world we inhabit. The harvest of a life lived in compassionate service is abundant, enriching not only the lives of those we serve, but our own lives as well, profoundly shaping our character and reflecting God's love within us.

COMPLIANCE

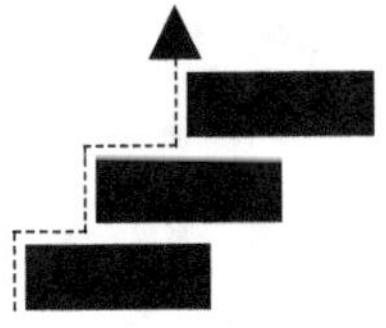

Chapter 3

Jesus' Disciples—A Model of Collaborative Ministry

The ministry of Jesus Christ wasn't a solo act. He didn't stride across the Galilean landscape healing the sick and preaching the good news all by Himself. No, He carefully cultivated a team, a fellowship of twelve men—His disciples—who learned from Him, worked alongside Him, and ultimately carried on His mission after His ascension. Their collaborative ministry provides a powerful model for effective teamwork, a model that resonates deeply with the challenges and opportunities faced by first responders and community personnel alike.

Consider the dynamics within this group of disciples. It wasn't a monolithic entity, a perfectly harmonized choir singing in unison. The disciples were individuals, each with their own personalities, strengths, and weaknesses. We see this vividly portrayed in the Gospels. Peter, impulsive and outspoken, often rushed ahead, sometimes to the detriment of the group's overall strategy. John, the beloved disciple, was known for his close relationship with Jesus and his insightful understanding of His teachings. Thomas, the doubter, challenged assumptions and demanded evidence. Judas, tragically, betrayed the trust placed in him. These are just a few examples of the diverse personalities that made up Jesus' team.

Yet, despite their differences, they all—minus Judas—continued to function as a team, a cohesive unit working towards a common goal. They learned from each other, supported each other, and compensated for each other's weaknesses. Jesus, as their leader, fostered this collaborative spirit. He didn't micromanage; He empowered them to take on responsibility, to use their individual gifts and talents for the advancement of the Kingdom. He delegated tasks, entrusting them with preaching the Gospel, healing the sick, and even performing deliverances.

He provided guidance, instruction, and correction, but He allowed them the space to grow, to learn through experience, and to develop their own unique ministries within the larger context of His overall mission.

This isn't just a historical observation; it's a blueprint for effective teamwork in any field, especially in the demanding environments faced by first responders and community personnel. Think about the challenges you face daily: the need for clear communication under pressure, the coordination of efforts in complex situations, the importance of mutual support and encouragement, the necessity of relying on the expertise of your colleagues. The disciples' model offers practical insights into navigating these very challenges. Their success, their failures, and their ultimate triumph all provide valuable lessons on the crucial role of teamwork.

Jesus' approach to leadership is particularly relevant. He didn't demand obedience through fear or coercion; He inspired loyalty through love, service, and example. He was present alongside His disciples, sharing their burdens, celebrating their successes, and offering comfort in their times of despair. His leadership style cultivated a sense of shared purpose, a feeling that they were all part of something bigger than themselves. This sense of collective identity, of shared mission, is vital for creating strong, effective teams. When team members feel valued, respected, and understood, when they are empowered to contribute their unique skills and talents, they are more likely to work together effectively, to overcome obstacles, and to achieve their common goals.

The Gospels provide numerous examples of this collaborative ministry. The feeding of the five thousand (Matthew 14:31-21), for instance, involved the disciples actively participating in the miracle. They weren't merely passive observers; they were integral to the event, distributing the bread and fish, and witnessing firsthand the power of Jesus' ministry. The same principle applies to the numerous healing miracles described in the Gospels. The disciples often played a key role in identifying the sick, preparing them for healing, and witnessing the transformative power of Jesus' touch.

Even the seemingly mundane tasks of their ministry, such as traveling from town to town, preaching the Gospel, and caring for the needs of the people, required effective teamwork. They shared responsibilities, relying on each other for support, encouragement, and practical assistance. They were a traveling ministry team, constantly working together, adapting to new situations, and solving problems collectively. Their ability to function as a team despite their inherent differences underscores the strength and resilience of a well-coordinated group. This is a lesson that resonates powerfully with the need for effective collaboration in community service. No single person, however skilled or dedicated, can effectively address the multifaceted challenges faced by our communities. We need to work together, pooling our resources, expertise, and energy to achieve meaningful and lasting positive change.

Furthermore, the challenges faced by the disciples offer a potent reminder of the importance of resilience and perseverance. Their ministry was not without its trials and tribulations. They faced opposition from religious authorities, persecution from the Roman Empire, and personal struggles that tested their faith and commitment.

Yet, they persevered, drawing strength from their shared faith, their mutual support, and their unwavering belief in Jesus' mission. Their resilience underscores the necessity of building strong support networks within teams. The ability to share burdens, offer encouragement, and provide practical assistance is crucial for sustaining morale and preventing burnout in the demanding fields of emergency response and community service. Just as the disciples drew strength from their bonds of fellowship, so too must first responders and community personnel cultivate strong relationships of support and encouragement within their teams.

The disciples' experience also highlights the importance of clear communication and effective coordination. Their successes and failures alike demonstrate the critical role of open and honest communication in overcoming obstacles and achieving their goals. When communication breaks down, when individuals act independently, or when there is a lack of coordination, the potential for disaster increases dramatically. This principle is paramount in emergency situations, where clear and concise communication can be the difference between life and death. The ability to share information swiftly and efficiently, to coordinate actions, and to adapt strategies in response to changing circumstances is essential for effective management. This same principle applies to community service, where the effective coordination of resources and efforts is key to achieving meaningful and sustainable progress.

Finally, the ministry of the disciples underscores the importance of shared leadership. While Jesus was the ultimate leader, He empowered His disciples to take on responsibility and to exercise leadership within the context of their collective mission. This sharing of authority not only enhanced efficiency but also fostered a sense of ownership and commitment among the team members. Everyone felt valued, respected, and empowered to contribute to the overall success of the ministry. This is an essential element of strong team dynamics.

When individuals feel valued and empowered, when they have the opportunity to contribute their unique talents and expertise, they are more likely to be engaged, committed, and effective team players. Sharing leadership also helps prevent burnout, distributing the weight of responsibility and ensuring that all members of the team are actively contributing to their success. The disciples' ministry offers a compelling example of how shared leadership can enhance teamwork, increase efficiency, and foster a sense of ownership and commitment among team members.

In conclusion, the collaborative ministry of Jesus and His disciples serves as a powerful and enduring model for effective teamwork in all fields of service, particularly in the demanding work of first responders and community workers. Their example highlights the importance of shared purpose, mutual support, clear communication, effective coordination, and shared leadership. By understanding and applying the principles exemplified in the disciples' ministry, we can build stronger, more effective teams, capable of addressing the challenges and opportunities of service with greater effectiveness, resilience, and impact. Theirs is a story that transcends time and context, offering timeless wisdom and practical guidance for building strong, effective, and compassionate teams that serve their communities with courage, compassion, and unwavering commitment to teamwork.

The Dangers of Self-Deployment— Lessons from the Gospels

The Gospels are replete with stories illustrating the dangers of self-deployment, a lesson tragically relevant to both the ministry and the world of first responders. Jesus, the ultimate leader, didn't operate in a vacuum. He consistently emphasized the importance of teamwork, even in seemingly solitary acts of ministry. Consider the story of the paralytic lowered through the roof in Mark 2:1-12. While the faith of the friends carrying the man was pivotal, their collaborative effort was essential for the miracle to occur. Had one of them faltered, had they not collectively found a way to overcome the obstacles presented by the crowd and the building's structure, the healing would not have taken place. This emphasizes that even seemingly individual acts of faith or service rely on the support structure of a team.

The temptation to act alone, to "go rogue," is a powerful one. It stems from a desire to be a hero, to demonstrate individual strength and capability. But this very impulse can be a dangerous trap. The Gospels show us time and again how acting outside of established protocols or without the support network of a team can lead to both ineffective ministry and significant personal risk.

Take, for example, the various instances of Jesus sending His disciples out in pairs. This wasn't mere redundancy. It was a calculated strategic decision based on safety, mutual support, and the principle of accountability. Two sets of eyes are better than one, two sets of hands are stronger than one pair, and two hearts sharing a burden can sustain far greater stress than one. This strategy also mirrors the best practices in law enforcement, where officers are rarely deployed individually, especially in high-risk situations. The buddy system is not just a guideline; it's a cornerstone of operational safety. It's a recognition of the shared vulnerability inherent in fieldwork, and the necessity of mutual support and backup.

The consequences of self-deployment can be devastating. We see echoes of this in the Gospels, albeit in a less directly physical form. Consider the story of Peter's denial of Jesus (Luke 22:54-62). In a moment of fear and isolation, he acts alone, separating himself from the support of the other disciples. This individual act of denial has repercussions far beyond his personal crisis; it reflects the fragility of faith when not anchored in community and the strength that emerges from mutual accountability. In the context of first responders, a similar scenario might involve one attempting to handle a situation beyond their training or capabilities, leading to injury, death, or a compromised outcome. The isolation inherent in self-deployment strips away the vital support system of a team.

The necessity of adhering to established protocols is another crucial element. Jesus, even with His divine authority, operated within the framework of the Heavenly Father's will (John 6:38). This respect for authority isn't simply a matter of obedience; it's a recognition of the wisdom and experience embedded in established systems. These systems aren't just rules and regulations; they represent the collective wisdom garnered from years, even centuries, of experience, lessons learned from successes and failures. In law enforcement and emergency services, protocols are not arbitrary; they are the product of rigorous research, analysis of incidents, and the accumulated knowledge of countless individuals who have faced similar situations.

To disregard these protocols is to ignore the wisdom of the past, to risk repeating mistakes, and to jeopardize safety and effectiveness. A law enforcement example vividly illustrates this point. Imagine a lone officer responding to a domestic disturbance call without backup, ignoring established protocol regarding minimum response numbers. The officer might be injured or even killed because of lacking the support needed to handle an unpredictable, potentially violent situation. The risks are heightened without the mutual support and backup afforded by a team. This example clearly demonstrates the consequences of acting outside established guidelines and prioritizing individual heroism over teamwork and safety.

Furthermore, the principle of chain of command is paramount. In the military, law enforcement, and even in the ministry, effective operations rely on a clear hierarchy of authority and responsibility. Jesus, while demonstrating incredible authority and independence, did not operate outside the will of His Heavenly Father. His example underscores the significance of respecting the structure of authority within a team. This structure is not about control; it's about clear communication, effective coordination, and ultimately, a safer and more efficient operation. Ignoring the chain of command can lead to chaos, confusion, and a breakdown in communication. This could result in missed opportunities for intervention or even exacerbate the situation, leading to more significant harm. In emergency services, clear communication and coordination are paramount. A lack of adherence to the chain of command could mean critical information isn't passed effectively, resulting in delays in response time or misallocation of resources. This underscores the potentially fatal consequences of ignoring established protocols and procedures.

In conclusion, the Gospels offer a powerful lesson in the dangers of self-deployment. Jesus' ministry, while characterized by extraordinary acts of power and compassion, was always rooted in teamwork and adherence to established guidelines. His example, coupled with the realities of modern law enforcement and community service, underscores the paramount importance of working within a team, respecting the chain of command, and adhering to safety protocols.

The temptation to act alone, to prioritize individual heroism over collective safety, is a powerful one; but it is a temptation that must be resisted. The lessons from the Gospels and the experiences of first responders and community personnel alike show us that true strength lies not in solitary action, but in the collaborative power of a team working together, guided by wisdom, experience, and a shared commitment to service. It is in this collaborative spirit that we find the most effective as well as the safest path to achieving our goals and serving our communities effectively. The call to service is not a solo act; it's a chorus of voices working together in harmony.

Building Effective Teams— Strategies for Collaboration

The parable of the Good Samaritan isn't just about individual compassion; it's a testament to the power of coordinated response. The Samaritan encountered the injured man alone. He single-handedly lifted him onto a donkey, transported him to the inn, and paid for his care; but he needed the support of the inn keeper to complete the mission.

The Samaritan's actions, while profoundly compassionate, were also a demonstration of the inherent need for collaborative effort in emergency situations. This principle holds true in every facet of community service and responses. We are called to be the hands and feet of Christ, and those hands and feet work most effectively when coordinated in purposeful action. Hanging in my office is a poster with an acrostic for the word TEAM as Together Everyone Achieves More.

My experience as an Emergency Services Chaplain taught me this lesson early on. Responding to a high-risk situation, whether a domestic dispute escalating into violence or a large-scale emergency, demanded a level of coordination and teamwork that was breathtaking.

A single person, no matter how brave or skilled, is at a significant disadvantage. The coordinated response of many, each with specific roles and responsibilities, drastically improves the likelihood of a successful and safe resolution. It's about understanding one another's strengths and weaknesses, anticipating each other's moves, and operating as a well-oiled machine—a team united by purpose.

This kind of teamwork doesn't just spring forth organically. It demands intentionality, planning, and ongoing effort. Building effective teams requires a deliberate strategy. First, clear and open communication is paramount. Those in the field rely on constant, concise updates. A missed radio call, an unclear command, or a breakdown in communication can have devastating consequences. This extends beyond simply relaying information; it includes active listening, empathetic understanding, and ensuring that everyone feels heard and valued. It's about recognizing that the value of a team comes not just from individual skill but from the synergy of skills combined, and the knowledge that each member plays a crucial role.

In community service settings, this translates into regular team meetings, transparent reporting, and consistent feedback mechanisms—all vital components of maintaining an open line of communication that ensures everyone is on the same page.

Conflict is inevitable in any team setting. Even within the most tightly knit groups, disagreements arise, personalities clash, and misunderstandings occur. However, it's how these conflicts are handled that truly defines the team's effectiveness. A well-functioning team isn't conflict-free; it's conflict-competent. It has established methods for resolving disputes constructively. In my years of service, I saw teams successfully navigate disagreements through structured mediation, clear communication, and a commitment to finding solutions that benefit the group as a whole.

The ability to address conflict head-on, respectfully, and directly is crucial for building trust and strengthening team bonds. Suppressing conflict only serves to create deeper resentment and ultimately undermine the team's unity and effectiveness. We learned that resolving conflict involved not winning an argument but finding common ground and understanding opposing viewpoints.

Effective teamwork also demands shared leadership. While a formal chain of command is essential for maintaining order and accountability, the best teams also cultivate a sense of shared responsibility. Everyone contributes their unique skills, insights, and perspectives. Leadership isn't limited to a single person or title; it's a collaborative effort where individuals take initiative, offer support, and mentor one another. In my work with community service groups, I witnessed the power of shared leadership firsthand. In a collaborative environment, the strength of the entire unit is multiplied, because each individual feels empowered to contribute, lead, and support their team members.

Mutual respect forms the bedrock of any successful team. It's not about superficial politeness; it's about truly valuing each member's contributions, respecting their perspectives, even when they differ from our own, and celebrating each other's successes.

This means creating an environment where everyone feels safe to express their ideas without fear of judgment or ridicule. It means acknowledging individual strengths and providing support where weaknesses exist. A truly respectful team fosters a culture of trust and empathy, where individuals feel valued, supported, and empowered to reach their full potential. This supportive environment is especially crucial in high-stress situations, where mutual support can be the difference between success and failure, between life and death.

Building effective teams is not a one-time event; it's an ongoing process. It requires constant attention, consistent effort, and a commitment to fostering a positive and productive team culture. Regular team-building activities, both formal and informal, can significantly enhance morale and collaboration. These activities can range from simple icebreakers and social gatherings to more intensive exercises designed to improve communication and problem-solving skills. They provide opportunities for team members to interact outside of work and to build stronger personal connections, which can translate into increased trust and improved working relationships. In the context of my work, team-building exercises not only strengthened individual bonds but also improved the efficiency and success of emergency response protocols.

Furthermore, it's crucial to recognize and reward team achievements. Individual recognition is important, but celebrating collective successes reinforces the sense of shared purpose and accomplishment. This can take many forms—a simple "thank you," a public acknowledgment at a meeting, or a more formal award or commendation. When a team feels appreciated and valued, they are more likely to remain engaged, motivated, and committed to achieving their goals. The recognition of teamwork is a tangible way to show appreciation and solidify the cooperative spirit within the team.

Finally, effective teams are constantly evolving and adapting. As circumstances change, as new challenges emerge, teams must be able to adjust and refine their strategies. This requires flexibility, a willingness to learn and grow, and an openness to new ideas. Regular evaluations of team performance, constructive feedback, and a willingness to implement changes based on that feedback are all critical components of building and maintaining a high-performing team. This involves a constant feedback loop to ensure everyone is on the same page, understands their roles and responsibilities, and feels empowered to contribute meaningfully to the team's mission.

The principles of effective teamwork extend far beyond the realm of law enforcement and community service. They are essential for success in any field where collaboration is key. Whether in a church group, a business organization, or a family, the principles of open communication, conflict resolution, shared leadership, mutual respect, and continuous improvement are fundamental to building strong, cohesive, and highly effective teams. It is through this collaborative spirit, modeled in the lives of those who serve faithfully, that we can truly embody the spirit of Christ's teachings and make a lasting impact on the world around us. The ultimate goal is not merely efficiency, but the creation of a supportive environment where each member flourishes and the whole is greater than the sum of its parts. This is the foundation of a team guided by faith, strengthened by collaboration, and empowered by a shared sense of purpose.

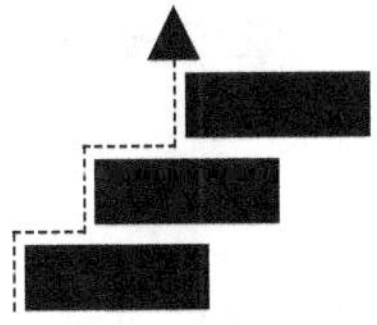

Chapter 4

Communications and Coordination in High-Pressure Situations

The Samaritan's journey wasn't just a solo act of kindness; it was a coordinated response, albeit an impromptu one. He found the victim, assessed the situation, secured aid, and facilitated the transfer of care. This seemingly simple act highlights the critical role of communication and coordination, even in spontaneous emergency responses. In structured environments like law enforcement and community service, these elements are not merely beneficial—they're paramount to success and, often, survival. Imagine a fire rescue, a hostage situation, or a large-scale natural disaster. The chaos, the fear, the sheer volume of variables demands a level of organized communication that is beyond merely effective; it must be flawless. Otherwise, lives are put at risk.

Clear, concise communication in high-stress environments isn't just about using the right words; it's about understanding the nuances of effective communication under pressure. This requires rigorous training and constant practice. Think about the clarity needed for a dispatcher receiving a frantic 911 call. Every word, every hesitation, every piece of information relayed—all of these impact the speed and efficacy of the response. Ambiguity can be deadly. A simple miscommunication about location, the number of victims, or the nature of the emergency can lead to delays, putting lives at risk and potentially hindering the rescue operation.

For example, consider the scenario of a multi-vehicle accident on a busy highway. First responders need to communicate the severity of the injuries, the number of patients, the need for additional resources (ambulances, fire trucks, hazmat teams), and the safest route to access the accident site while ensuring public safety.

Simultaneously, they must communicate with hospital staff to prepare for the influx of patients, inform traffic control to manage the flow of traffic and prevent secondary accidents, and ensure that communication reaches the families of the victims. This requires seamless integration between multiple teams and agencies, each with their own protocols and communication systems.

The established protocols—the standardized operating procedures—aren't merely bureaucratic hurdles; they are the lifelines in chaotic situations. They ensure uniformity and interoperability. They provide a framework that enables different agencies to work together seamlessly, regardless of their background or training variations. Imagine a scene involving multiple agencies: police, fire, EMS, and perhaps even disaster response teams. Each has its own jargon, its own methods of operation, its own communication systems.

However, the existence of a unified command structure and established protocols ensures that they don't operate in silos. They work as a cohesive, interdependent system, united by a common goal: to mitigate the emergency, save lives, and protect property.

Effective communication in these environments relies heavily on active listening. In the midst of chaos, it's easy to focus solely on transmitting information. However, active listening—truly hearing and understanding what others are saying, acknowledging their contributions, and responding appropriately—is just as important.

This is where empathy plays a critical role. Responding to a frantic family member amidst a crisis requires not just the delivery of factual information but also compassion and understanding. Active listening involves paying attention to non-verbal cues as well, which can often be more telling than the spoken word. A subtle shift in body language or a change in tone might indicate a critical piece of information that could be easily missed if one isn't actively listening. Beyond active listening, the concept of situational awareness is crucial. Team members must constantly scan the environment, assessing the evolving circumstances, identifying potential threats, and adapting their communication and actions accordingly.

A sudden shift in the wind during a wildfire, an unexpected surge of bystanders at a crime scene, or a change in the behavior of a suspect during a negotiation—these are all critical changes that demand immediate adjustments in communication strategy.

Training plays a significant role in honing these skills. Simulated exercises and real-life scenarios allow responders to practice working together, communicating effectively, and reacting appropriately under pressure. These exercises are designed to mimic the stress and unpredictability of real emergencies, helping responders to build their resilience and improve their communication skills. They also highlight potential weaknesses in communication protocols, allowing for adjustments and improvements to the system. Constant feedback and continuous improvement are essential parts of this process. Regular drills and debriefing sessions after significant incidents allow for identification of best practices and areas where improvement is needed.

Technology also plays a crucial role in enhancing communication and coordination. Modern communication systems, including two-way radios, mobile data terminals, and integrated dispatch systems, enable rapid information exchange, real-time location tracking, and efficient resource allocation. These technological advancements significantly improve the efficiency and safety of response efforts, especially during large-scale emergencies where many agencies and individuals might be involved. However, technology is only as good as the people who use it. Proper training on the use of these systems, along with robust maintenance and backup plans, are essential to avoid reliance on technology that may fail at the most critical moment.

The efficiency of communication can be significantly enhanced by the use of clear, concise language. Jargon, slang, and ambiguous terminology should be avoided to prevent misinterpretations. Instead, clear, precise, and standardized language should be employed, especially when communicating with multiple agencies or personnel with diverse backgrounds and levels of experience. This includes the use of plain English, avoiding unnecessary technical terms, and adhering to predetermined communication protocols. This promotes understanding and reduces the risk of errors.

Beyond formal communication channels, informal communication also has its place. The trust and camaraderie among team members can facilitate quick, efficient communication during a crisis. A simple nod, a gesture, or a glance can communicate crucial information faster than a lengthy radio transmission. This informal communication, built upon a foundation of mutual respect and shared understanding, adds another layer of efficiency to the team's responses. It is the unspoken understanding that develops through rigorous training, constant interaction, and a shared commitment to the mission.

Finally, the importance of post-incident analysis cannot be overstated. After each emergency, whether major or minor, a thorough review of the communication and coordination aspects is essential. This includes analyzing communication logs, reviewing body-worn camera footage, and conducting debriefing sessions with all involved personnel. This process serves to identify areas for improvement, refine protocols, and strengthen the team's ability to handle future emergencies. This continuous cycle of learning and adaptation is critical to maintaining a high level of preparedness and efficiency. It's a testament to a team's commitment to excellence, constantly striving to be better, to serve more effectively, and to honor the calling they have embraced. The goal is not merely survival, but success—success in saving lives, in protecting communities, and in upholding the values that guide their service. It's a ministry of action, reflecting the selfless love of the Good Samaritan and the unwavering dedication of those who answer the call to serve.

Teamwork and Spiritual Unity— A Shared Purpose

The Samaritan's parable isn't merely a story of individual compassion; it's a blueprint for effective teamwork. His actions, though spontaneous, demonstrate a synergy of assessment, resourcefulness, and coordinated action. This same principle, the necessity of unified effort, resonates deeply within the structured environments of law enforcement and community service, and even more powerfully within the context of our shared faith.

The success of any endeavor, be it rescuing a victim from a burning building or building a thriving community, hinges upon a shared understanding, mutual respect, and a common, unwavering purpose.

My years spent serving within the community, both as a first responder and as a chaplain, have profoundly underscored this truth. I have witnessed firsthand the breathtaking power of unified action, the transformative potential that blossoms when individuals lay aside personal ambitions and embrace a collective vision. It's not simply about coordinating tasks; it's about weaving together hearts and minds, creating a tapestry of purpose that is far greater than the sum of its parts. This synergy, this spiritual unity, is the very essence of effective teamwork. It's the bedrock upon which we build our communities, and it's a testament to the power of faith working in concert with action.

Consider the Apostle Paul's powerful metaphor of the body in 1 Corinthians 12: "Just as a body, though one, has many parts, but all its many parts form one body, so it is with Christ." This isn't a mere analogy; it's a profound spiritual truth reflecting the interconnectedness within the body of Christ, mirrored in the collaborative spirit needed for effective teamwork. Each member, with their unique gifts and talents, contributes to the overall well-being and functionality of the whole.

Just as a hand cannot function without the arm, or the foot without the leg, so too can individual members within a team struggle to thrive without the support and collaboration of their fellow members. This interdependence is a powerful illustration of the spiritual unity needed for a truly effective team.

In law enforcement, this principle is paramount. Imagine a SWAT team breaching a building. The success of the operation doesn't rest on the individual prowess of a single officer, but on the precise, coordinated actions of the entire unit. Each member has a specific role, a defined task, yet their actions are inextricably linked. A failure in communication, a moment of hesitation, a lack of trust—any of these can lead to disastrous consequences. This level of synchronization requires more than training; it requires a profound trust in one another, a belief in the team's shared capability, a recognition of the shared responsibility. This, in essence, is spiritual unity in action. It's a testament to the belief that each member is essential, each contribution valued, each person's strength complementing the strengths of others.

This resonates deeply with my experiences within the church. I have seen firsthand how a shared faith, a common dedication to service, can transform a diverse group of individuals into a unified, highly effective team. We are called not only to serve the Lord but to serve our community. Our church's motto in Key West, Florida, is "Committed to Our Community." To live out this motto requires collaboration, planning, and a constant reassessment of how we can best meet the needs of those around us.

Whether it's organizing a food drive, providing disaster relief, or simply offering a listening ear to a troubled neighbor, the success of these endeavors depends on the collective effort, the shared commitment to a common goal. The spiritual dimension of teamwork extends beyond simple cooperation; it delves into the realm of shared values.

A strong team is built not merely on shared tasks but on shared beliefs. When individuals are united by a common purpose, infused with a spirit of service, their collective power is amplified exponentially. It's a dynamic of synergy, where the whole is far greater than the sum of its parts. This is not a mystical notion; it's a demonstrably effective approach to both secular and spiritual endeavors. In the context of faith, this shared purpose is rooted in our love for God and our commitment to serving others as reflections of His love.

This shared understanding, however, isn't always easily achieved. Teams, like any human endeavor, are susceptible to internal conflict, misunderstandings, and personality clashes. These challenges, however, are not insurmountable. Through diligent work, open communication, and a commitment to resolving conflicts through empathy and understanding, we can build a stronger, more unified team.

Just as a skilled conductor harmonizes the various instruments of an orchestra, creating a powerful and beautiful symphony, so too can effective leadership harmonize the diverse talents and perspectives within a team. Effective leadership in this context is not about dominance or control; it's about servant leadership—a model championed by Jesus Himself (John 13:1-17). It's about empowering individuals, fostering collaboration, and creating an environment where every member feels valued and respected. It's about recognizing and leveraging the unique strengths of each member, creating a synergistic effect where the whole is greater than the sum of its parts. This requires empathy, patience, and a willingness to listen and learn from the experiences of others. It's about recognizing that each member brings unique skills and perspectives to the team, and that these differences are not weaknesses but strengths to be celebrated and leveraged.

Furthermore, the role of prayer in strengthening team unity cannot be overstated. Collective prayer, when offered with sincerity and humility, can create a powerful bond amongst team members. It's a reminder that our work is not simply our own; it's a collaboration with God, a shared journey guided by faith and mutual support.

This shared spirituality becomes a source of strength, encouraging resilience in the face of challenges and fostering a

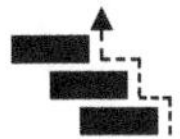

deep sense of camaraderie. This is a spiritual glue that strengthens the bonds of the team and ensures that the team remains focused on its shared purpose. I often sit in my office and hear my wife Shena praying with the volunteers and clients serving and being served at our food pantry.

The principles of teamwork are not merely theoretical constructs; they are essential for effective community service and law enforcement, as well as profoundly relevant to our spiritual lives.

The parable of the Good Samaritan is a powerful reminder that true service often requires a coordinated effort, a collaboration of individuals working together towards a common goal. In the same vein, building a strong, effective team within any context—religious, professional, or community-based—requires a concerted effort to establish shared values, cultivate spiritual unity, and foster a culture of mutual respect and collaboration. The pursuit of shared purpose is an ongoing process, a journey of continuous growth and learning.

It's about actively striving to understand each other's perspectives, to overcome our differences, and to leverage our collective strengths to achieve our common goals. It's about embracing the diversity within the team, recognizing that each member brings unique talents and perspectives, and fostering an environment where everyone feels valued and respected.

This shared purpose, rooted in our faith, guides, and empowers us to serve our communities effectively. It provides a framework for understanding our roles and responsibilities within the larger context of our shared humanity. It allows us to see beyond our individual limitations and to focus on the collective good.

Ultimately, it's a reminder that we are all connected, that our successes and failures are inextricably linked, and that by working together, in unity and with faith, we can accomplish far more than we ever could alone. This shared purpose is the very foundation of effective teamwork, the cornerstone of a thriving community, and a reflection of God's love in action.

It's a living testament to the power of collaboration, guided by faith and propelled by a shared commitment to serve. The journey is not always easy, but the rewards—the lives touched, the communities strengthened, the faith deepened—are immeasurable. It's a ministry of action, a reflection of the selfless love of the Good Samaritan, and a testament to the power of teamwork guided by faith.

PERSONAL AUDIT

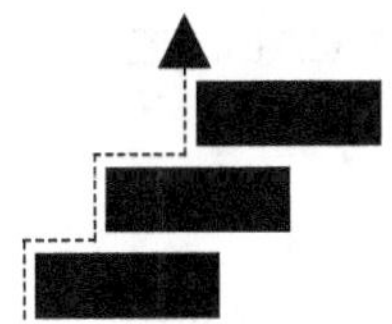

Steps to Success
Personal Audit

Jesus modeled and gave us vivid examples of courage, compassion, and compliance. These three traits or steps are needed for effective service.

I have provided here a personal audit aimed at assisting you in evaluating and improving your steps to success in these three traits. Please read each of the following statements. Circle the number that best describes how true each statement is of you.

COURAGE

1. I always run toward response situations fraught with emotion.

    1. True

    2. More true than false

    3. More false than true

    4. False

2. I have the faith that gives me the courage to face fears.

    1. True

    2. More true than false

    3. More false than true

    4. False

3. My courage is seen in my creativity under pressure.

    1. True

    2. More true than false

    3. More false than true

    4. False

4. I am always mentally prepared for my deployments.

    1. True

    2. More true than false

    3. More false than true

    4. False

5. I am totally committed to cultivating a continuous process of learning, adapting, and growing.

    1. True

    2. More true than false

    3. More false than true

    4. False

COMPASSION

1. I have mastered the traits of the ministry of presence.

    1. True

    2. More true than false

    3. More false than true

    4. False

2. I am satisfied with my level of emotional intelligence.

    1. True

    2. More true than false

    3. More false than true

    4. False

3. I always treat myself with the same kindness and understanding I extend to others.

    1. True

    2. More true than false

    3. More false than true

    4. False

4. I constantly practice self-reflection with a commitment to confront my biases and prejudices.

    1. True

    2. More true than false

    3. More false than true

    4. False

5. I always strive to treat others how they want to be treated.

    1. True

    2. More true than false

    3. More false than true

    4. False

COMPLIANCE

1. I always lay aside personal ambitions and embrace the collective vision.

    1. True

    2. More true than false

    3. More false than true

    4. False

2. I always work with the team, pooling my resources, expertise, and energy to achieve meaningful and lasting positive change.

    1. True

    2. More true than false

    3. More false than true

    4. False

3. I always provide guidance, instruction, and correction, but allow my team the space to grow, to learn through experience.

    1. True

    2. More true than false

    3. More false than true

    4. False

4. I fully understand the dangers of self-deployment, and always adhere to the no self-deployment rule.

    1. True

    2. More true than false

    3. More false than true

    4. False

5. I always recognize and leverage the unique strengths of each member of the team.
    1. True
    2. More true than false
    3. More false than true
    4. False

TOTAL YOUR SCORE

Total the number of times you gave each answer and place that total in the spaces provided, then multiply by the given numbers for your total points for each answer.

1. # of True answers = _______ x 1 = _______ points

2. # of More true than false answers = _______ x 2 = _______ points

3. # of More false than true answers = _______ x 3 = _______ points

4. # of False answers = _______ x 4 = _______ points

Add the total points from 1-4 to calculate your Total Score.

TOTAL SCORE: _____________

AUDIT RESULTS BASED ON YOUR TOTAL SCORE

15–25 | Courage, compassion and compliance are ingrained in your personal life and leadership role.

26–35 | You are practicing the three steps. If your total score is closer to 35, you need to pay more attention to one or more of the steps.

36–45 | You need to continue to work on developing all three steps.

46–60 | Others probably do not view you as being effective in your role. You may want to take some time to rethink your motives for service.

PERSONAL IMPROVEMENT STEPS

The purpose of this exercise is to focus on identifying areas that need improvement and developing a plan for the same.

STEP ONE: Choose one statement under the category of COURAGE that you answered using a 3 or 4, and write it out below.

____

____

____

____

My score for this statement is (circle one):   3   4

STEP TWO: Develop a plan for personal improvement.

PERSONAL DEVELOPMENT PLAN

1. ____

____

____

____

2. ____

____

____

____

3. ____

____

____

____

PERSONAL IMPROVEMENT STEPS

The purpose of this exercise is to focus on identifying areas that need improvement and develop a plan for the same.

STEP ONE: Choose one statement under the category of COMPASSION that you answered using a 3 or 4, and write it out below.

____

____

____

____

My score for this statement is (circle one):   3   4

STEP TWO: Develop a plan for personal improvement.

PERSONAL DEVELOPMENT PLAN

1. ____

____

____

____

2. ____

____

____

____

3. ____

____

____

____

PERSONAL IMPROVEMENT STEPS

The purpose of this exercise is to focus on identifying areas that need improvement and develop a plan for the same.

STEP ONE: Choose one statement under the category of COMPLIANCE that you answered using a 3 or 4, and write it out below.

____

____

____

____

My score for this statement is (circle one):   3   4

STEP TWO: Develop a plan for personal improvement.

PERSONAL DEVELOPMENT PLAN

1. ____

____

____

____

2. ____

____

____

____

3. ____

____

____

____

You have now completed your steps to success personal audit. As you begin to implement your developmental plan, it will be wise to be patient and remember this process may be repeated as necessary.

FAITH-BASED INITIATIVES

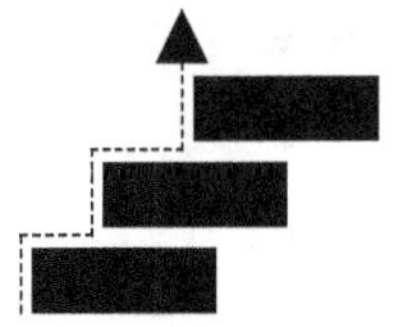

Chapter 5

The Intersection of Faith and Community Engagement

The profound connection between faith and community engagement isn't merely a matter of pious pronouncements; it's the very heartbeat of a life lived authentically. For those of us who find our strength and purpose in our faith, service to others isn't an optional add-on; it's an intrinsic expression of our beliefs. The scriptures consistently emphasize compassion, justice, and love for our neighbors—a call to action that echoes through the centuries and resonates deeply within the human spirit. This isn't a vague, abstract concept; it's a tangible reality played out in countless acts of service, big and small, across the globe.

Consider again the parable of the Good Samaritan. This isn't just a story about extending kindness to a stranger; it's a powerful illustration of crossing boundaries, overcoming prejudices, and acting on a deep-seated commitment to compassion. The Samaritan, a member of a despised group, chooses to show mercy where others would turn away, a testament to the power of faith to transcend cultural and social divides. His actions are a powerful challenge to our own biases and a call to extend grace to those who might seem "unworthy" of our help. In the context of community engagement, this means recognizing the inherent dignity of every individual, regardless of background, circumstance, or perceived social status. It means seeing the face of Christ in the faces of those we serve (Matthew 25:40).

This principle is echoed throughout the New Testament, prompting us to actively participate in alleviating suffering and promoting justice. Jesus' ministry wasn't confined to preaching sermons; it was characterized by tangible acts of service—healing the sick, feeding the hungry, and advocating for the oppressed. He didn't merely talk about love; He embodied it, demonstrating the inseparable link between faith and action. His example sets a powerful precedent for all who claim to follow Him, calling us to engage in active service as a direct manifestation of our faith. This isn't about earning salvation through good works; rather, it's about allowing our faith to inform and guide our actions, shaping us into individuals who are genuinely committed to making a difference.

The impact of faith-based community initiatives is undeniable. Across nations, countless organizations—churches and other faith-based institutions—are on the front lines of addressing social issues, providing vital services, and strengthening communities. These groups often step into gaps where government services are lacking or insufficient, providing a critical lifeline to those most in need. From food banks and homeless shelters to after-school programs and disaster relief efforts, the contributions of faith-based organizations are transformative, often reaching people in profound and meaningful ways. They aren't simply offering material assistance; they are providing a sense of belonging, hope, and dignity.

For many, the motivation to serve stems directly from their faith. The belief that all humans are created in God's image instills a profound sense of respect and responsibility toward our fellow human beings. The conviction that we are all interconnected and part of a larger community compels us to care for those who are vulnerable and marginalized. This conviction doesn't leave room for indifference or apathy; it fuels a deep-seated desire to actively participate in building a more just and compassionate world. This isn't a passive faith; it's a faith that compels action, a faith that is lived out in the daily routines and challenges of community service.

However, faith-based community engagement is not without its challenges. Inherent tensions exist between the desire to serve and the need to respect the diverse beliefs and perspectives of those we serve. Sometimes, our well-intentioned efforts may be perceived as intrusive or culturally insensitive, highlighting the need for humility, sensitivity, and a deep understanding of the communities we serve. This requires active listening, a willingness to learn, and a genuine commitment to building bridges rather than walls. Success demands that we actively engage in cross-cultural dialogue, seeking to understand diverse perspectives rather than imposing our own.

The importance of building bridges between different communities is paramount. This involves actively fostering inclusivity and developing respectful relationships that transcend differences in religion, ethnicity, or socioeconomic status. In our increasingly diverse society, the ability to build bridges is essential for effective community engagement. It requires self-reflection, a willingness to challenge our own biases, and a commitment to creating spaces where everyone feels welcome, valued, and respected.

Our faith calls us to see the divine image in every individual, regardless of background or belief. Consider the countless examples of faith-based organizations that have successfully navigated the complexities of community engagement. They have not only provided essential services but also built lasting relationships with the people they serve, fostering a sense of community and belonging.

Their commitment to building trust and mutual respect has allowed them to serve effectively, building relationships that transcend religious affiliation. They demonstrate that faith-based service is not a separate domain but an integral part of fostering strong, vibrant communities.

The experiences of many first responders and community service personnel testify to the power of faith in providing strength, hope, and resilience in the face of adversity. In situations characterized by high stress and emotional trauma, faith can provide an anchor in the storm, offering a sense of purpose and meaning. For many, it's not merely a source of comfort; it's a driving force that enables them to continue serving despite the challenges they face. It provides resilience, hope, and a profound sense of meaning in the often difficult and demanding world of emergency services.

It's crucial to recognize that faith isn't a cure-all for all the problems that plague our communities. It's not a magical solution to complex societal issues. Rather, it's a powerful source of motivation, inspiration, and resilience, providing the foundation for meaningful and impactful community engagement. It's a source of strength that allows individuals to face challenges head-on, to persevere in the face of setbacks, and to continue serving those most in need.

Ultimately, the intersection of faith and community engagement is a powerful force for positive change. It's a call to action, a challenge to live out our beliefs in tangible ways, and an opportunity to make a real difference in the lives of others

and in the world around us. It is a testament to the belief that our faith should not be a private matter confined within the walls of a church or temple but should be expressed through acts of service, compassion, and love for our fellow human beings. This integration of faith and action is not merely desirable; it is essential for creating a more just, equitable, and compassionate world.

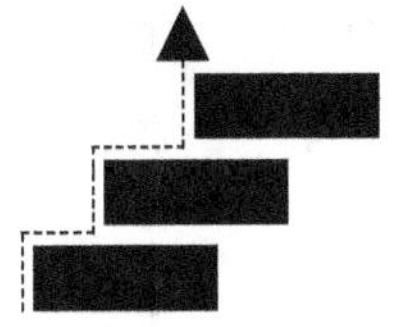

Chapter 6

Faith-Based Initiative
Best Practices

The transformative power of faith-based initiatives is undeniable. Across diverse communities, religious organizations have consistently demonstrated a remarkable capacity to address complex social issues, offering practical solutions and fostering genuine human connection. However, several programs have faltered due to a lack of clear strategic planning and measurable goals. In the late 1990s as a member of an international delegation of forty persons selected by their respective nations, we visited twelve USA cities in thirty days and were introduced to best practices for faith-based initiatives. I am eternally grateful to the Government of The Commonwealth of The Bahamas for selecting me for this life and service-influencing opportunity.

The group came to realize that without a defined roadmap and specific, achievable objectives, efforts can become diffuse and ultimately ineffective. Decades later, I am still benefiting from principles learned and gleaned on that trip. Here are a few.

I can't over emphasize the importance of developing a comprehensive strategic plan, complete with measurable goals and regular evaluation processes. A program focused on improving literacy rates, for example, needs specific, quantifiable targets and regular assessments to track progress and identify areas for improvement. Otherwise, the initiative might drift, lacking the focus and accountability needed to achieve lasting impact.

A common pitfall is a failure to involve the community directly in the design and implementation of programs. Top-down approaches, where initiatives are imposed on the community rather than developed in collaboration with them, often fail to achieve lasting change. Community ownership is critical for sustainable success. Genuine participation allows for a deeper understanding of the local context, cultural sensitivities, and the specific needs of the community members. This collaborative approach can significantly enhance the initiative's relevance and increase its chances of achieving lasting impact. For instance, a program aimed at reducing crime might fail if it doesn't incorporate the insights and perspectives of the community members most affected by crime.

The financial sustainability of faith-based initiatives is also a critical factor. Many organizations struggle with securing consistent and adequate funding. This makes it crucial to develop diverse funding strategies, including grants, fundraising events, and community partnerships. The development of sustainable funding models is paramount for long-term success. Reliance on solely one funding stream can be precarious. Diversifying funding sources reduces risk and enables ongoing operation even in challenging economic times. For example, a program supporting vulnerable families might benefit from a combination of grants, corporate sponsorships, and individual donations, ensuring its stability and capacity to continue offering vital services. I firmly believe in the four streams approach for financially stabilizing an initiative (Genesis 2:10–14).

In evaluating the effectiveness of faith-based initiatives, we must move beyond simply counting numbers. While quantifiable

metrics like the number of people served or jobs created are important, it is equally essential to assess the qualitative impact. This includes measuring changes in community cohesion, social capital, individual empowerment, and overall well-being. Collecting qualitative data, through interviews, focus groups, and observations, can provide a deeper understanding of the initiative's impact. This holistic approach encompasses not only immediate results but also the long-term effects on individuals, families, and the community as a whole. For instance, a mentoring program for at-risk youth should not only track the number of youths mentored but also assess the positive changes in their academic performance, social behavior, and overall sense of hope and purpose. Initiatives with measurable outcomes have the data necessary for positive adjustments.

Furthermore, effective faith-based initiatives often excel at fostering partnerships. Collaboration with other organizations, government agencies, and community leaders amplifies impact and extends reach. By building a broad network of support, these initiatives can access more resources, expertise, and reach a wider range of beneficiaries. A program focusing on environmental conservation, for example, might collaborate with local environmental agencies, schools, and businesses to maximize its impact and create a more comprehensive approach to environmental stewardship.

In conclusion, the effectiveness of faith-based initiatives hinges on several key elements: a clearly defined strategic plan, genuine community engagement, sustainable funding models, a holistic evaluation approach, and strong partnerships. By understanding and implementing these best practices, faith-based organizations can amplify their positive impact and create meaningful, lasting change within their communities.

The common thread woven through all successful initiatives is a deep commitment to serving others, coupled with a pragmatic and adaptable approach to problem-solving. These are not just charitable acts; they are investments in the well-being of communities, fostering resilience, hope, and a brighter future for all. The work continues, and the lessons learned from both successes and failures pave the way for even greater positive change in the future. The integration of faith and service is a powerful engine for societal betterment and a testament to the enduring power of compassion, dedication, and a belief in the inherent worth of every individual.

Overcoming Challenges—Addressing Conflicts and Misunderstandings

The transformative power of faith, as we have explored, extends far beyond the walls of a church. Its influence resonates deeply within the fabric of community service, providing both motivation and a framework for positive action. However, the very act of integrating faith into service can, at times, introduce complexities. Differences in beliefs, interpretations, and approaches can lead to conflicts and misunderstandings, potentially hindering the effectiveness of even the most well-intentioned initiatives. Navigating these challenges requires sensitivity, understanding, and a commitment to respectful dialogue.

One common area of friction arises from differing perspectives on the nature and purpose of service itself. Some may view service as a purely secular act, focusing on tangible outcomes and measurable impact. Others may see it as an expression of faith, an opportunity to live out their religious beliefs through tangible action. This divergence can create tension, particularly when

decisions are made regarding resource allocation, program design, or the prioritization of specific needs.

For instance, consider a faith-based organization providing assistance to individuals experiencing homelessness. Some members might prioritize providing spiritual guidance alongside material support, believing that addressing the spiritual needs is crucial for holistic healing and transformation. Others, perhaps more focused on immediate practical needs, might advocate for prioritizing shelter, food, and job training, viewing spiritual matters as secondary or even potentially intrusive. Resolving this conflict requires open communication, empathy, and a willingness to find common ground. It might involve creating separate tracks within the program, ensuring that individuals can receive support that aligns with their personal preferences and beliefs. This approach respects diverse perspectives while ensuring that everyone benefits from the program's services.

Another area of potential conflict stems from differing interpretations of religious teachings. Even within the same faith tradition, significant variations in understanding specific doctrines or ethical principles can exist. These differences can affect how individuals approach service initiatives, leading to disagreements on issues like inclusivity, outreach strategies, and even the very definition of 'good works.'

Let's imagine a food bank operated by a predominantly conservative Christian organization. A debate might arise over food options for other religious community members. While some might argue that offering these options is essential for inclusivity and fulfilling the organization's mandate to serve all those in need, others might express concerns about conflicting with their interpretation of biblical teachings. Successfully resolving this requires a deep understanding of the various viewpoints, engaging in respectful dialogue, and recognizing the importance of respecting cultural and religious diversity. This could involve carefully educating participants on the diversity of beliefs and adjusting practices to better accommodate diverse dietary needs.

Beyond internal conflicts, disagreements can also arise between faith-based organizations and secular entities. These may involve differing views on the separation of church and state, the role of religious institutions in public life, or even the suitability of faith-based approaches to address specific social problems.

For example, a faith-based organization running an after-school program might face resistance from school officials who are hesitant to incorporate religious elements into the curriculum, fearing a violation of the separation of church and state. Navigating this requires careful adherence to legal guidelines and a commitment to transparent and inclusive practices. The solution might involve offering separate faith-based activities outside of the school's mandated curriculum or adapting the program to focus on universally accepted values that resonate with diverse religious and non-religious individuals.

The key to overcoming these challenges lies in fostering a culture of respect, empathy, and open communication. Leaders of faith-based organizations must create spaces where diverse perspectives are welcomed, valued, and incorporated into decision-making processes. This requires active listening and a commitment to finding mutually acceptable solutions.

Training programs for volunteers and staff can be invaluable in equipping individuals with the skills and knowledge needed to navigate these delicate situations. Such training should emphasize conflict resolution techniques, interfaith dialogue, and an understanding of relevant legal and ethical considerations.

Role-playing exercises can be particularly effective in preparing individuals for real-world scenarios.

Moreover, establishing clear communication protocols and guidelines can help prevent misunderstandings from escalating into conflicts. Regular meetings, open forums, and feedback mechanisms can provide opportunities for individuals to voice their concerns, share their perspectives, and work collaboratively towards solutions.

It is crucial to remember that disagreements are not necessarily indicative of failure. Rather, they often present valuable opportunities for growth, learning, and strengthening community bonds. When handled constructively, conflicts can lead to a deeper understanding of diverse perspectives, ultimately enhancing the effectiveness and impact of faith-based service initiatives. The process of resolution should be seen as an integral part of the service journey itself, a testament to the resilience and adaptability of both the organization and the individuals involved. By embracing diversity, fostering dialogue, and remaining committed to serving others, faith-based organizations can overcome challenges and achieve remarkable positive change in the world. Indeed, these challenges themselves often serve to refine and strengthen the very fabric of the organization, creating a more inclusive and effective engine for serving humanity. The successful navigation of these challenges becomes a testament to the organization's commitment to its founding principles and a beacon for others to follow. This resilience and adaptability, learned through the crucible of conflict, are hallmarks of a truly impactful and lasting community service organization.

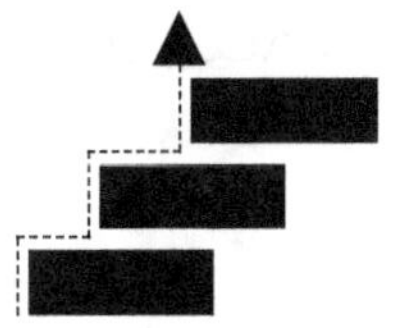

Chapter 7

Building Bridges That Foster Inclusive and Respectful Relationships

We have explored some of the challenges inherent in integrating faith and service, the potential for friction when differing beliefs and approaches collide. But the beauty of faith-based service lies precisely in its ability to transcend these differences, to become a unifying force rather than a divisive one. This requires a conscious and deliberate effort to build bridges—to foster inclusive and respectful relationships that celebrate diversity while upholding shared values of service and compassion. This isn't simply about tolerance; it's about genuine embrace.

My own experience in disaster response and community chaplaincy taught me a valuable lesson about the power of understanding different perspectives. Responding to calls, often in crisis situations, forced me to interact with people from all walks of life—people struggling with addiction, poverty, mental health issues, and so much more. Initially, my approach was often rooted in a "by the book" mentality, a procedural approach that didn't always account for the human element. I quickly learned that we are not to treat others how we wish to be treated but rather how they want to be treated. It meant seeing the individual, not just the circumstance. This shift in perspective was transformative, not just for my effectiveness as a responder, but for my own spiritual growth. It broadened my empathy and deepened my understanding of the complexities of human experience.

This principle applies equally, if not more intensely, to faith-based service organizations. We cannot simply preach tolerance; we must actively practice it. We must create spaces where individuals from different backgrounds, beliefs, and experiences feel safe, respected, and valued. This requires a proactive approach, a conscious effort to cultivate inclusivity at every level of our service organizations.

One practical strategy is to actively seek diverse perspectives in the planning and implementation of service projects. Too often, well-intentioned initiatives are conceived and carried out within a homogeneous group, leading to projects that may not effectively address the needs of the broader community. By actively involving individuals from diverse backgrounds in the design process, we ensure that the projects are not only effective but also relevant and culturally sensitive. This might involve establishing advisory boards comprised of representatives from various community groups, conducting thorough needs assessments that consider the unique circumstances of different populations, or simply engaging in open dialogue with community leaders and members.

For example, when our church decided to launch a food bank, we didn't simply assume what the community needed. We held meetings with different community stakeholders. We listened to concerns, and by incorporating this feedback, we ended up not just with a community food bank, but a vibrant hub of activity that brought together people from diverse backgrounds, forging relationships and fostering a sense of shared ownership. Publix Super Markets, Inc. has been our community partner for more than a decade and counting. This wasn't just about feeding individuals and families; it was also about growing community partnership dynamics.

Another key element in building bridges is fostering open and respectful communication. This means creating a safe space for dialogue, and especially when discussing sensitive or controversial topics. It requires active listening, the ability to truly hear and understand another person's perspective, even if we don't agree with it. It demands empathy, the capacity to step into another person's shoes and see the world from their point of view. And it requires humility, the willingness to acknowledge our own biases and limitations.

In our community service efforts, we have encountered situations where differing interpretations of religious texts or ethical principles have led to conflict. Instead of shying away from these disagreements, we have learned to embrace them as opportunities for learning and growth. We have found that respectful dialogue, facilitated by skilled mediators, when necessary, can help bridge divides and foster a deeper understanding of different perspectives. It's not about finding a single "correct" answer, but about fostering mutual respect and understanding.

For instance, we once faced a disagreement within our group regarding the appropriate way to approach individuals experiencing homelessness. Some advocated for a direct, interventionist approach, providing immediate assistance and resources. Others preferred a more indirect, relational approach, building trust and rapport before offering assistance. Initially, these different approaches seemed diametrically opposed, threatening to fracture our group. However, through facilitated dialogue, we were able to understand the rationale behind each approach and appreciate the strengths and limitations of each.

Ultimately, we synthesized these different approaches, developing a more comprehensive and effective strategy that incorporated the best elements of both. This process not only resolved the conflict but also strengthened our group's internal cohesion and deepened our capacity for collaborative action.

Furthermore, the principles of inclusivity should extend to the very structure and governance of faith-based service organizations. Ensuring that leadership roles are diverse and reflect the community served is crucial. This isn't simply about representation; it's about ensuring that decision-making processes are informed by diverse perspectives and experiences. It's about fostering a culture of shared power and ensuring that the voices of all members are heard and valued.

This might involve implementing mentorship programs to support individuals from underrepresented groups in assuming leadership positions, establishing clear guidelines for equitable representation on decision-making bodies, or conducting regular reviews of organizational policies and practices to identify and address potential biases. Some organizations have adopted a system of rotating leadership roles, ensuring that everyone has the opportunity to contribute to the organization's governance and decision-making. This often fosters a greater sense of ownership and shared responsibility, further strengthening the sense of community.

Building bridges also extends to understanding and actively addressing systemic issues that create barriers to inclusion. This might involve advocating for policies that promote equal access to resources, challenging discriminatory practices within institutions, or working to dismantle systemic inequalities that perpetuate marginalization. It requires us to look beyond the immediate needs of our service projects and to consider the broader social,

economic, and political contexts that shape the lives of the communities we serve.

Our faith calls us not only to act charitably, but also to strive for justice. For example, in working with a community struggling with high rates of unemployment and limited access to education, we realized that simply providing immediate relief through food banks or housing assistance was not a sustainable solution. We partnered with local organizations to advocate for policies that would increase job training opportunities and improve access to education, working towards systemic change that would address the root causes of poverty and inequality.

Finally, building bridges requires a commitment to ongoing learning and self-reflection. We must constantly strive to expand our understanding of different cultures, perspectives, and experiences. This means actively seeking opportunities for cross-cultural learning, engaging in conversations with individuals from diverse backgrounds, and critically examining our own biases and assumptions. It's a lifelong process of growth and development, a journey that requires humility, perseverance, and a genuine desire to learn and grow.

The journey toward building truly inclusive and respectful relationships is not a destination, but a continuous process of learning, adapting, and growing together. It is a testament to the transformative power of faith, not just in our individual lives, but in the lives of the communities we strive to serve. Through intentional effort, we can transform potential conflict into opportunities for growth, strengthening the fabric of our community and enriching the lives of all.

Faith as a Source of Strength and Resilience in Service

The relentless nature of community service often leaves individuals feeling depleted, emotionally drained, and questioning their commitment. The weight of unmet needs, the pervasive suffering, and the sheer scale of the problems can be overwhelming. It's in these moments, when the road ahead seems impossibly long and arduous, that faith emerges as a lifeline, a wellspring of strength and resilience that sustains us through the darkest hours. My own journey, bridging my background in emergency services with my unwavering faith, has repeatedly underscored this truth.

For years, I served at-risk youth and their families, witnessing firsthand the stark realities of poverty, violence, and despair. The challenges were immense, the victories often small and fleeting. Days bled into weeks, weeks into months, and the cumulative effect took its toll. Burnout loomed like a constant threat, a dark cloud threatening to obscure the purpose that had initially fueled my dedication. It was my faith, my deep-rooted belief in God, which anchored me during those turbulent times. It wasn't a passive faith; it wasn't a mere belief in a distant God. Rather, it was a living, breathing relationship, a constant source of solace and strength.

Prayer wasn't just a ritualistic act performed at the start and end of the day; it became a continuous dialogue with God, a way of sharing my burdens, fears, anxieties, and hopes. In those moments of intense pressure, when the weight of responsibility seemed unbearable, prayer served as a powerful release, allowing me to surrender my anxieties to a power far greater than myself. It was during these prayers that I found a renewed sense of purpose, a reaffirmation of my commitment to serving others.

The Bible was my vital source of guidance and inspiration. Passages like Psalm 23, "The Lord is my shepherd, I shall not want," resonated deeply, offering comfort and reassurance amidst the chaos and uncertainty. The stories of biblical figures—Moses leading his people out of slavery, David confronting Goliath, Esther bravely facing adversity—became beacons of hope, reminding me that, even in the face of seemingly insurmountable obstacles, faith can provide the courage and strength to persevere.

The support of my faith community was also crucial. Surrounded by fellow believers, I wasn't alone in my struggles. Their prayers, words of encouragement, and shared experiences provided a sense of belonging and solidarity. We supported each other, carried each other's burdens, and celebrated each other's victories. This collective strength, this unwavering faith shared amongst a community, was a powerful antidote to the isolation and despair that often accompany community service.

But faith isn't just about overcoming personal challenges; it's also about finding the strength to serve others, even when those we serve don't share our faith. In my assignment, I encountered individuals from diverse backgrounds, many of whom held different beliefs or no religious faith at all. Yet, my faith didn't limit my ability to empathize with their struggles or offer compassionate service. Instead, it fueled my compassion, motivating me to treat each person with dignity and respect, regardless of their beliefs.

I recall a specific incident involving a young man caught in the cycle of addiction and crime. He was hardened, cynical, and deeply distrustful of authority figures. Initially, he resisted our attempts to help, his defenses firmly entrenched. Yet, through consistent, compassionate engagement—demonstrating a genuine concern for his well-being and showing unwavering respect—a connection began to emerge with both my staff and me. It wasn't about imposing my beliefs; it was about showing him the love and compassion that I believed were at the heart of my faith. Over time, a transformation took place. He began to share his story and to accept the support we were offering. Upon his graduation from the program, we were able to assist him in starting a small business comprised of selling roasted peanuts and phone cards on the street corner of a busy intersection.

Years later, while visiting my mother in the hospital, I saw a young man selling peanuts outside the hospital, which is a long-standing tradition in The Bahamas. I purchased three bags and told the vendor to keep the change. His response was "This has to be Mr. Carey!" Yes, it was my former student. He embraced me like I was a long-lost friend, and tears filled my eyes. In that moment of personal pain, his embrace lifted my spirit. I believe that the unwavering compassion rooted in my faith was a catalyst in his journey towards a healthier life.

This isn't to suggest that faith magically erases the hardships of community service. It doesn't eliminate the challenges, the setbacks, or the moments of despair. Instead, faith provides the inner strength, resilience, and unwavering hope necessary to navigate these difficulties. It's a source of perseverance, enabling us to continue serving even when our efforts seem futile, our resources depleted, and our spirits weary. The integration of faith and service isn't merely a matter of adding a spiritual dimension to an already existing framework; it's about fundamentally altering our approach to service. It's about moving beyond mere compassion to a profound and abiding love, fueled by a spiritual understanding of human worth and divine potential. It is about seeing each individual not simply as a case file or a statistic, but through the lens of God, deserving of our unconditional love and care.

Furthermore, this faith-based approach necessitates humility and a willingness to learn. It requires that we acknowledge our limitations and turn to God for guidance and strength. It compels us to constantly evaluate our own actions and motives, ensuring that our service is driven by genuine love and compassion rather than personal ambition or self-aggrandizement.

The strength derived from faith also fosters empathy and understanding. It helps us see beyond the surface-level manifestations of suffering and recognize the deeper spiritual and emotional wounds that contribute to individuals' struggles. This deeper understanding enables us to approach our work with a greater degree of sensitivity and compassion, offering not just practical solutions, but also emotional support and spiritual guidance.

In conclusion, the integration of faith in community service isn't a peripheral element; it's foundational. It provides a bedrock of resilience, a boundless source of hope, and a profound impetus for service. Through the lens of faith, the arduous tasks of service become acts of worship, the challenges become opportunities for growth, and the service itself becomes a profound expression of love for God and humanity. My journey, marked by both the challenges of community service and the unwavering strength of faith, has shown me time and time again that this integration isn't merely an ideal, but a powerful reality, capable of transforming both the lives of those we serve and our own. It's a transformative power that extends beyond the individual, enriching communities and leaving an enduring legacy of hope and compassion. The resilience that stems from faith is not merely personal; it's a force that strengthens our communities and, ultimately, the world.

Personal Transformation Through Service— The Author's Journey

My journey into emergency services wasn't a calling born from a childhood dream of disaster responses and the like. It stemmed from a deeper, more unsettling place—a place of witnessing injustice firsthand in my own community. Growing up in a small island of various communities, I saw firsthand the struggles of families caught in cycles of poverty, addiction, and despair. I watched families under the weight of unemployment and illness, their dreams slowly eroding under the harsh realities of life. These weren't abstract societal problems; they were my neighbors, my friends, people I knew. This ignited within me a desire, a burning need, to be a part of the solution, however small.

Later, as I transitioned into pastoral and community service roles, this perspective deepened significantly. I volunteered at our Fellowship's summer camps, assisted with community cleanup projects, and mentored at-risk youth. Each interaction, no matter how seemingly insignificant, was a powerful reminder of the human spirit's resilience and capacity for hope. I learned the importance of listening, truly listening, without judgment or preconceived notions. I saw the transformative power of empathy and understanding, how a simple act of kindness could restore faith and hope in the human heart. These weren't just tasks; they were opportunities to build relationships, to foster trust, and to contribute to a better future for my community.

The transition from primarily reacting to crises in my pastoral role to proactively helping build strong and healthy communities through service was profound. It changed my perception of my own capabilities and my sense of purpose. In the late 90s, I was appointed a member of The Bahamas National Crime Commission and overnight became a part of a larger collaborative structure. My work on the crime commission involved collaborating with individuals from different backgrounds, each possessing unique skills and experiences. Together, we crafted crime reduction strategies, spearheaded community outreach programs, and fostered collaborations across diverse social groups and community organizations. This approach went beyond simply reacting to crime; we actively built a framework of prevention, collaboration, and community support. This experience taught me the importance of diversity in problem-solving. Different perspectives and experiences brought valuable insights to the table. We learned to leverage each other's strengths, to overcome individual limitations through collective action, and to achieve results that none of us could have accomplished alone. The success of the crime commission wasn't just measured by crime statistics; it was measured in the strengthened relationships, the restored trust, and the renewed sense of hope that permeated the community.

These experiences fundamentally reshaped my understanding of service. It wasn't simply about "doing my job," but about embodying a spirit of service that permeated every aspect of my life. It's about recognizing the intrinsic value in every human being, regardless of their circumstances, and actively seeking ways to uplift and empower them.

The transformative power of selfless giving is not merely an abstract concept; it's a palpable, life-altering experience. The act of serving others, of offering a helping hand, of sharing time and resources, unlocks a deep sense of purpose, fulfillment, and joy. It challenges us to step outside of ourselves, to focus on the needs of others, and to recognize our shared humanity. This, in turn, cultivates empathy, compassion, and a stronger sense of belonging within our community. The more I served, the more I found myself transforming.

My own anxieties and insecurities began to fade as I focused on the needs of others. My perception of my own value shifted from an egocentric perspective to one of shared human connection and responsibility.

The journey has also shown me that service is not limited to grand gestures or heroic acts. The most profound transformations often come from small, everyday acts of kindness—a listening ear, a helping hand, a word of encouragement. These seemingly insignificant actions can have a ripple effect, creating positive change that extends far beyond the immediate interaction. They are the building blocks of a stronger, more compassionate world.

It's important to remember that this journey is not a linear path; it is a process of continuous growth and learning. There will be setbacks, challenges, and moments of self-doubt. But the very act of serving others provides the resilience to persevere. The relationships built, the trust established, and the knowledge that we are making a difference sustain us through those difficult times and reinforce our resolve to continue serving.

I believe that everyone possesses a unique set of gifts and talents, a capacity for service that, if embraced, can transform not only the lives of others but also our own. It is my hope that sharing this journey will inspire you to discover and nurture your own capacity for service, to find your place in the tapestry of community, and to experience the profound transformation that comes from a life dedicated to serving others. The journey is often challenging, demanding both physical and emotional resilience. Yet, the rewards—the connections forged, the lives touched, the communities strengthened—far outweigh any personal sacrifice.

It's a journey of continuous growth and self-discovery, a path that leads to a deeper understanding of ourselves and our place in the world. It's a path upon which I encourage you all to embark.

The Ripple Effect of Compassionate Action— Long-Term Impacts

We often underestimate the power of a single act of kindness. We might offer a helping hand, a listening ear, or a simple word of encouragement, thinking it's a small gesture, easily forgotten. But the truth is, these seemingly insignificant actions create ripples, expanding outwards to touch countless lives in ways we can scarcely imagine. This is the transformative power of compassionate service—not just in the immediate impact, but in its enduring legacy. Consider my example of serving as the principal of Program SURE on Grand Bahama Island in The Bahamas. I was asked by the Ministry of Education in 1993 to develop a school for at-risk male students. Program SURE (Success Ultimately Reassures Everyone). In the second year of the school's existence, a female student approached me and asked to attend. With it being a male-only school, I had to convince the district school superintendent that she would be safe in the environment and that we would be sensitive to all necessary protocols. She successfully completed the program and moved on with her life.

In 2011, I received a call on Facebook Messenger from the young lady thanking me for taking a chance on her. She went on to explain that she was married with two children, working as a nurse, and involved with helping girls in need of mentors. It was a great reminder of the importance of faith and works (James 2:14–26).

The ripple effect extends beyond the immediate recipients of our service. Think about the volunteers at a local soup kitchen. They're not just feeding the hungry; they're creating a sense of community, providing a moment of human connection in the midst of hardship. This interaction, often fleeting, can reignite a spark of hope, reminding individuals that they're not alone in their struggle. Moreover, the act of volunteering itself inspires others to get involved. Witnessing the compassion of others often motivates individuals to engage in service themselves, creating a chain reaction of kindness that spreads throughout the community.

This transformative power isn't confined to large-scale initiatives. The ripple effect can be seen even in the smallest acts of compassion. Holding the door open for someone, offering a seat to an elderly person on the bus, or lending a helping hand to a stranger carrying heavy groceries—these simple and seemingly insignificant gestures can brighten someone's day, making them feel seen, valued, and cared for.

These small interactions can alleviate stress, boost morale, and even inspire a recipient to pay it forward, perpetuating a cycle of kindness. I remember a time when I was assisting a woman who had been a victim of domestic violence. She was understandably apprehensive, frightened, and deeply vulnerable. The simple act of offering her a cup of tea, listening to her story without judgment, and reassuring her that she wasn't alone made a tangible difference. She found strength in our conversation, a strength she carried with her, helping her navigate the difficult journey ahead. Her resilience, in turn, empowered her to support others in similar situations, proving that the impact of one compassionate action can extend far beyond the initial interaction.

The long-term impact of compassionate service goes beyond the immediate benefits for individuals. Stronger communities are built on empathy, collaboration, and shared responsibility. When we invest in our communities through service, we are not just helping others; we are building a stronger social fabric. We foster a sense of belonging, promoting social cohesion and reducing isolation. This, in turn, has far-reaching consequences for public safety, economic stability, and overall well-being. By investing in our communities through compassionate service, we are also investing in our own future.

This notion extends beyond our immediate surroundings. Our globalized world highlights the interconnectedness of all humanity. Acts of service extended across geographical boundaries, like supporting international aid organizations or contributing to global health initiatives, have a profound and far-reaching impact. These efforts often address systemic issues, promoting sustainable development, poverty reduction, and improved healthcare in underserved regions. The contribution, however small it may seem individually, contributes to a larger collective effort to create a more just and equitable world.

The transformative power of service is not limited to any particular field or profession. It's a universal principle applicable to all aspects of life. Whether you're a teacher, a doctor, a lawyer, an artist, or a homemaker, you have the potential to make a significant difference in the lives of others through your actions. The key lies in recognizing your own unique abilities and talents, and actively seeking opportunities to use those skills to serve others. This isn't about grand gestures or heroic actions; it's about consistent, everyday acts of kindness, empathy, and generosity.

Moreover, the benefits of service are not one-sided. While we often focus on the positive impact our actions have on others, we must also acknowledge the profound personal transformation that comes from a life dedicated to service. Engaging in acts of compassion fosters personal growth, enhancing our self-awareness, empathy, and resilience. The experience of connecting with others on a deeper level brings a sense of purpose and meaning to our lives, often leading to increased happiness and overall well-being. This personal transformation, in turn, enables us to serve with greater effectiveness and passion.

The journey of service is not always easy. It requires dedication, patience, resilience, and the willingness to face challenges. We will experience moments of frustration, disappointment, and even burnout. Yet, these experiences are integral parts of the journey, shaping us, strengthening us, and deepening our commitment to serving others. The rewards far outweigh the challenges; the deep connections forged, the lives touched, the communities strengthened—these are the enduring legacies of a life dedicated to compassionate service.

Therefore, I urge you to embrace the transformative power of service. Discover your unique abilities and talents, identify areas where you can make a difference, and take the first step. Whether it's volunteering at a local charity, mentoring a young person, or simply offering a helping hand to a neighbor, your actions have the potential to create ripples of change that extend far beyond your immediate reach. Let us build a world where compassionate service is not an exception, but the norm, a world where each individual recognizes their inherent capacity to make a profound and lasting difference.

Let us embark on this journey of service together, creating a tapestry of kindness and compassion that transforms both ourselves and the world around us. This is not just a call to action; it's a call to a deeper, more fulfilling life. A life where each of us discovers the transformative power of serving others and, in doing so, transforms ourselves.

Building Stronger Communities—
The Role of Collective Action

We have explored the profound impact of individual acts of service, the ripples of kindness spreading outwards to touch countless lives. But the transformative power of service isn't solely about individual efforts; it's amplified exponentially through collective action. Think of it like this: a single drop of water might barely make a dent, but a torrent of rain can reshape landscapes. Similarly, the combined efforts of many individuals, working together with a shared vision, can create monumental positive change within our communities.

This isn't merely about adding more hands to a task; it's about synergizing strengths, leveraging diverse skills, and fostering a sense of shared ownership and responsibility.

The strength of a community lies not just in its individual members, but in the intricate web of relationships, support systems, and collective endeavors that bind them together. When we work together, we tap into a reservoir of resources, both tangible and intangible, far exceeding what any single individual could accomplish alone. This collective action isn't just about efficiency; it's about building a stronger sense of community, fostering trust, and empowering individuals to become active participants in shaping their own destinies.

Consider neighborhood watch programs. They are not just about crime prevention; they're about building a network of trust and mutual support. Neighbors get to know each other, look out for one another, and create a safer, more secure environment. This collective vigilance fosters a sense of shared responsibility, transforming a neighborhood from a collection of individuals into a cohesive community where everyone feels valued and protected.

The success of collective action hinges on effective communication and collaboration. This requires open dialogue, mutual respect, and a willingness to listen to diverse perspectives. Differences in opinion are not weaknesses; they're opportunities for growth and innovation. By embracing these differences and learning from one another, communities can develop more comprehensive and effective solutions to their challenges.

Effective collaboration requires strong leadership, but not necessarily in the traditional sense. Leadership in collective action often emerges organically, from individuals who possess a particular skill, passion, or ability to inspire and motivate others. These leaders might not hold formal positions of authority, but they exert significant influence through their dedication, commitment, and ability to build consensus. It's about empowering individuals to take ownership of their roles, fostering a sense of shared responsibility and ensuring that every voice is heard.

One of the most impactful forms of collective action is volunteerism. Volunteering provides a powerful platform for individuals to contribute their time, talents, and energy to causes they care about. Whether it's assisting at a local soup kitchen, mentoring underprivileged youth, or participating in environmental cleanup efforts, volunteering builds stronger communities by providing much-needed support and fostering a sense of shared purpose. It strengthens social connections, builds bridges across different social groups, and promotes a sense of civic responsibility.

The impact of collective action extends far beyond individual projects and initiatives. It contributes to the overall social fabric, fostering a sense of shared identity and community spirit. This sense of shared identity is crucial for building strong, resilient communities capable of weathering challenges and emerging stronger. When individuals feel connected to their community and invested in its well-being, they are more likely to participate actively in its growth and development.

However, collective action is not without its challenges. Differences of opinion, competing priorities, and logistical hurdles are inevitable. Overcoming these challenges requires patience, understanding, and a commitment to finding common ground. Open communication, clear goals, and well-defined roles are essential to ensure that collective efforts remain focused and productive.

Moreover, successful collective action requires recognizing and addressing power imbalances within the community. It's imperative to ensure that marginalized groups have a voice and are actively involved in decision-making processes. Inclusive participation is not just a matter of fairness; it's crucial for developing solutions that address the diverse needs and concerns of the entire community.

Ignoring the needs of marginalized groups not only undermines the effectiveness of collective action but also perpetuates existing inequalities. Furthermore, sustainability is a critical consideration in collective action. Simply initiating a project or program is not enough; sustained effort is essential to create lasting positive change. This requires careful planning, resource management, and a long-term vision that extends beyond immediate gains. Building strong communities is a marathon, not a sprint, and collective action needs to be viewed as a continuous process of engagement, adaptation, and refinement.

Building strong communities through collective action requires a commitment to both the immediate and the long term. It requires a vision of a better future, a willingness to work collaboratively, and a deep understanding of the interconnectedness of individuals and their environment. By embracing the transformative power of service through collective action, we not only enhance the well-being of our communities but also enrich our own lives. We discover the profound satisfaction that comes from working together towards a common goal, fostering a sense of shared purpose and creating a legacy of positive change that extends far beyond our own lifetimes. This shared journey fosters empathy, understanding, and a deeper appreciation for the interconnectedness of our lives, ultimately leading to stronger, more resilient, and more compassionate communities. Let us strive to be not just members of a community, but active architects of its future, building a world where collective action is the norm, and where the transformative power of service reshapes our world for the better.

Inspiring Others to Serve— Passing the Torch

The transformative power of service, as we have seen, isn't a solitary endeavor. It's a wildfire, ignited by a single spark, but fueled by the collective breath of countless souls. We have explored the profound impact of individual acts, the ripple effect of kindness, the monumental shifts achieved through collaborative action. But the true legacy of service lies not just in the immediate impact, but also in the enduring flame passed from one generation to the next. It's about inspiring others to pick up the torch, to carry the flame of compassion and contribute to building a better world.

This isn't a passive process; it requires a proactive, intentional effort. It demands that we become not just servants, but mentors, leaders, and catalysts for change. We must inspire others to find their own purpose within the tapestry of service, to discover the deep satisfaction that comes from contributing to something larger

than themselves. How do we ignite this spark in others? How do we cultivate a culture of service that ripples through generations?

One of the most powerful tools we possess is the power of storytelling. Sharing personal anecdotes of service—the challenges overcome, the lives touched, the profound personal growth experienced—can be incredibly motivating. When we share our stories with authenticity and vulnerability, we create a connection, a bridge between our own experiences and the potential experiences of others.

These stories don't need to be grand epics; they can be simple narratives of kindness, small acts of compassion that illuminated a dark corner, a moment of selflessness that transformed a situation. These everyday miracles, recounted with genuine emotion, can resonate deeply and inspire action. Think about the impact of a veteran sharing experiences volunteering at a homeless shelter, their hard-won wisdom revealing the depth of human connection amidst the difficulties. Or a young mother recounting how a simple act of helping an elderly neighbor made a profound impact on her children, teaching them the value of compassion and empathy. These accounts, shared informally within families, churches, community groups, or even through social media, can create a chain reaction, inspiring others to contribute their own unique talents and time. A simple account paints a picture of compassionate service.

Beyond personal narratives, we need to actively cultivate a culture of service within our communities. This requires leadership, both formal and informal. Schools can integrate service learning into their curricula, creating opportunities for students to engage in meaningful projects and develop a lifelong commitment to service. Churches and religious organizations can foster a culture of giving and compassion, providing opportunities for their congregations to serve both within their communities and globally. Community organizations can provide clear pathways for individuals to volunteer their time and skills, matching them with projects that align with their interests and capabilities.

The key is to make service accessible and engaging. We need to break down barriers, dispel misconceptions, and demonstrate that service is not just about charity; it's about mutual growth, shared responsibility, and building a stronger, more connected community. It's about fostering a sense of belonging, where everyone feels valued and empowered to contribute. For instance, consider creating mentorship programs pairing experienced volunteers with newcomers, offering guidance and support, fostering a sense of community among those serving. Highlighting the impact of volunteer work through regular updates, testimonials, and public acknowledgment—creating tangible examples of the positive change volunteers help create—further reinforces the value of participation.

Moreover, we must celebrate the achievements of those who serve. Public recognition, awards, and even simple expressions of gratitude can go a long way in fostering a culture of appreciation and encouraging continued engagement. We must move away from a culture that views service as a burden and embrace a culture where service is recognized as a privilege, a source of fulfillment and mutual benefit.

Creating opportunities for diverse participation is critical. We need to ensure that service initiatives are inclusive, accommodating individuals of all backgrounds, ages, abilities, and interests. This might involve adapting projects to accommodate physical limitations, offering multilingual support, or providing transportation assistance. It's about creating a welcoming and supportive environment where everyone feels valued and empowered to participate.

Furthermore, we must actively address the systemic issues that create barriers to service. Poverty, lack of access to transportation, childcare challenges, and other societal inequities can prevent individuals from engaging in service, particularly those from marginalized communities. Tackling these systemic issues is crucial to creating a truly inclusive culture of service. Finally, fostering a legacy of service involves explicitly empowering the next generation.

By engaging young people in service from a young age, we instill in them a lifelong commitment to contributing to the betterment of society. This might involve creating age-appropriate volunteer opportunities, mentoring programs, or youth leadership initiatives. By providing them with the tools and support they need, we can ensure that the torch of service continues to burn brightly for generations to come.

Consider the long-term impact of involving school children in community gardening projects, teaching them about sustainable practices and the value of community sustenance, while also offering a practical outlet for service. Or imagine the lasting benefits of organizing a youth-led initiative to support a local animal shelter, allowing young people to develop leadership skills while fostering a lifelong love for animals and a commitment to their welfare. These types of projects not only serve the immediate need but also sow the seeds of future engagement.

In essence, inspiring others to serve is about creating a virtuous cycle—a ripple effect of kindness and compassion that spreads outwards, transforming not only our communities but also ourselves. It's about cultivating a spirit of generosity, promoting collaboration, and building a legacy of service that endures for generations. It's about recognizing that the true measure of a society is not its wealth or power, but its capacity for compassion and its commitment to lifting each other up. Let us work together to create a world where the transformative power of service is not just a fleeting ideal, but a vibrant, enduring reality. Let us all become architects of a future built on empathy, collaboration, and the unwavering commitment to serve. The reward is not just a better world for our children and grandchildren but a richer, more meaningful life for ourselves. Let us embrace this calling and pass the torch forward, confident in the power of collective action to transform our world for good.

A Legacy of Service— Long-Term Vision and Sustainability

The fire of service, once ignited, must be carefully tended. A single act of kindness, a moment of compassion, can indeed change a life. But the true measure of our impact lies in the enduring legacy we leave behind—a legacy that continues to burn brightly long after we're gone. This isn't about fleeting moments of charity; it's about building sustainable systems, nurturing future generations of servants, and ensuring that the transformative power of service remains a vibrant force in our communities for decades to come. This requires a long-term vision, a strategic approach, and a relentless commitment to fostering growth and resilience within our service initiatives.

One crucial element is developing robust organizational structures. Think of a mighty oak—its strength comes not from a single, fragile branch, but from its intricate network of roots, trunk, and limbs, each supporting the other. Similarly, successful service organizations need strong foundations: clear governance structures, transparent financial management, and a dedicated team of volunteers and staff. This isn't simply about paperwork; it's about establishing a framework that ensures accountability, efficiency, and long-term stability. A well-defined mission statement, regularly reviewed and adapted to evolving community needs, provides crucial direction. This requires ongoing evaluation and adaptation—a willingness to learn from both successes and failures, to refine strategies and to adjust to the changing landscape of community needs.

Furthermore, building a strong organizational culture is paramount. This culture should be infused with a spirit of collaboration, mutual respect, and a shared commitment to the organization's mission. Regular training and professional development opportunities for volunteers and staff are essential to maintain high standards of service and ensure that everyone feels valued and empowered. Open communication channels, opportunities for feedback, and a supportive environment cultivate a sense of belonging and foster a culture of continuous improvement.

When individuals feel connected to the mission and valued within the organization, they are more likely to remain committed over the long term. This sense of community extends beyond the organization itself, fostering partnerships with other groups and institutions, creating a network of support that enhances the impact of the service initiatives.

Financial sustainability is another key pillar. While initial funding may come from grants, donations, or fundraising events, long-term sustainability requires the development of diverse and reliable revenue streams. This might involve exploring grant opportunities, building strong relationships with donors, establishing endowment funds, or creating revenue-generating programs.

Transparency in financial management is crucial to maintain trust and accountability, ensuring that every dollar is utilized effectively and efficiently to further the organization's mission.

Diversification is key—relying solely on one funding source is risky, making the organization vulnerable to unforeseen circumstances. A multifaceted approach ensures resilience and reduces dependence on any single source of funding.

Beyond the organizational aspects, nurturing future leaders is critical to the long-term vision of service. Mentorship programs, leadership training, and opportunities for younger generations to take on increasing responsibility within the organization are essential.

Empowering the next generation to carry the torch forward ensures that the legacy of service continues to thrive. This involves not just transferring knowledge and skills but also fostering a deep understanding of the organization's values and mission. This transfer of leadership isn't just about succession planning; it's about cultivating a continuous cycle of growth and renewal. It is about creating a pipeline of dedicated individuals who are passionate about the mission and committed to serving their communities.

Moreover, fostering a culture of evaluation and continuous improvement is critical. Regularly assessing the effectiveness of programs and initiatives allows for adjustments to be made, ensuring that resources are being used efficiently and that the desired outcomes are being achieved. This evaluation process shouldn't be seen as a critique, but as an opportunity for growth and learning. Collecting data, analyzing trends, and seeking feedback from beneficiaries and stakeholders are all essential components of a robust evaluation system. This process enables organizations to remain agile and responsive to the changing needs of the communities they serve.

Finally, and perhaps most importantly, the long-term vision of service rests on the unwavering commitment of individuals.

It is the tireless dedication of volunteers, staff, and supporters that ultimately sustains the transformative power of service. This dedication is fueled by a deep sense of purpose, a belief in the organization's mission, and a shared commitment to making a difference in the lives of others. Nurturing this commitment requires creating a culture of appreciation and recognition, celebrating successes, and providing ongoing opportunities for growth and engagement.

By fostering a strong sense of community and shared purpose, organizations can inspire individuals to remain committed over the long term, ensuring that the legacy of service endures for generations to come. The sustainability of service isn't merely a matter of logistics; it's a spiritual endeavor. It's about building a legacy of compassion, a testament to the transformative power of human kindness. It's about creating a world where acts of service aren't isolated events, but the very fabric of our communities. It's about passing the torch, ensuring that the flame of compassion burns brightly for generations to come, lighting the way towards a better future for all. This is the legacy for which we strive—a world where service isn't just a noble pursuit, but an enduring testament to the best of humanity. A world where the ripple effect of kindness continues to expand, transforming lives and communities, leaving an indelible mark on the tapestry of time. It's a vision worth fighting for, a legacy worth building, a future worth inheriting.

Building this legacy requires not only a long-term perspective but a deep understanding of the ever-shifting landscape of community needs. We must be adaptable, responsive to change, and willing to innovate our approaches to service. Technological advancements, changing demographics, and evolving social issues all necessitate a dynamic and flexible approach to service delivery. This requires continuous learning, a willingness to embrace new strategies, and a commitment to collaboration with other organizations and stakeholders. The challenge is not just to maintain the current level of service, but to continually enhance and expand its impact, ensuring that the legacy we leave behind is not only sustainable, but also transformative.

In the realm of community service, innovation is not simply a luxury; it is a necessity. It's about finding creative solutions to persistent problems, adapting to emerging challenges, and finding new ways to engage people in service.

This could involve leveraging technology to reach wider audiences, developing innovative programs that address specific community needs, or finding creative ways to engage volunteers and donors. Innovation isn't just about developing new programs; it's about reimagining existing ones, improving efficiency, and maximizing impact. It's about constantly asking ourselves: how can we do better? How can we reach more people? How can we create a greater and more lasting impact?

The work of building a sustainable legacy of service is a marathon, not a sprint. It requires patience, perseverance, and an unwavering belief in the transformative power of human kindness. There will be challenges along the way, setbacks and disappointments. But the reward is far greater than any temporary difficulty—it is the knowledge that we are contributing to a better future for generations to come. It is the satisfaction of knowing that our work is not in vain, but a beacon of hope, illuminating the path towards a more just, compassionate, and equitable world.

The true measure of our success will not be found in the accolades or recognition we receive, but in the lasting impact our service has on the lives of others. It's about leaving a world that is slightly better than the one we inherited, a world where the spirit

of service thrives, and where future generations are empowered to continue the work, carrying the torch of compassion forward, and building upon the legacy of those who came before them. This is the true calling of service—to build a legacy that resonates through time, a legacy of hope, compassion, and enduring transformation. It is a legacy we can all help to create. Let us embrace this challenge, and together, build a future where the transformative power of service shines brightly for generations to come.

Identifying Your Unique Gifts and Talents

The journey to embracing your calling isn't a sprint; it's a marathon, a lifelong pilgrimage of self-discovery and selfless service. Before you can effectively answer the call to action, you must first understand the unique instruments God has placed in your hands—your gifts and talents. This isn't about boasting or self-aggrandizement; rather, it's about honest self-assessment, a crucial step in aligning your passions with purpose. Think of it like a finely tuned orchestra: each instrument plays a vital role, and the most beautiful symphonies arise from the harmonious blend of diverse sounds. Your unique gifts are your unique voice in that divine orchestra.

Many of you might feel overwhelmed at the prospect of identifying your gifts and talents. You might be thinking, "I'm just a simple person. I don't have any special skills." But I'm here to tell you that's not true. Every single one of you possesses inherent strengths and abilities, gifts uniquely tailored to contribute to God's grand plan. The key lies in recognizing and nurturing those gifts, much like a farmer cultivates fertile land.

One of the most powerful tools for identifying your gifts is introspection—a journey inward to discover your deepest passions and aptitudes. Take time for quiet reflection. Pray for guidance.

Ask yourself these vital questions: What activities bring you a deep sense of joy and fulfillment? To what tasks do you find yourself naturally drawn? In what areas do you consistently excel? These aren't necessarily the things you're best at, but the things that energize you, the things that leave you feeling a sense of purpose and accomplishment. Think about your past experiences. Perhaps you have always had a knack for problem-solving. Maybe you excel at comforting others during times of distress. Or perhaps you are naturally adept at organizing and coordinating events. These skills—honed through years of experience—are indicators of your innate talents. Don't discount the seemingly "small" things.

The ability to listen empathetically, the willingness to lend a helping hand, the simple act of offering a kind word—these are all invaluable gifts that can make a profound difference in the lives of others. Consider your natural inclinations. Are you outgoing and extroverted, thriving in environments where you can interact with many people? Or are you more introspective, finding satisfaction in solitary work that allows for deep contemplation and focus? Understanding your personality type can help you pinpoint areas where your gifts can flourish. If you're an extrovert, you might excel in roles that involve direct interaction and community outreach. If you're an introvert, you might be better suited for behind-the-scenes tasks such as administrative work or research.

Don't be afraid to ask for feedback from trusted friends, family, and mentors. Sometimes, we are blind to our own strengths, and others can offer valuable insights. Ask them what they see as your unique abilities and contributions. Their perspectives might surprise you, revealing hidden talents or strengths you never considered. Constructive criticism, if received with an open heart, can be a powerful tool for growth.

Remember the parable of the talents in Matthew 25. The master entrusts his servants with different amounts of talents (money) based on their abilities. He doesn't punish those who didn't earn massive returns; he punished the one who buried his talent, who failed to utilize what he was given. God has given each of us unique talents, and we are called to use them, to grow them, to share them with the world. The failure isn't in the lack of extraordinary results; it's in the failure to use what you have.

In my own experiences, I have seen firsthand how diverse talents are crucial in serving our community. One might excel at deescalation, using calm words and empathetic listening to resolve tense situations peacefully. Another might be a master investigator, adept at piecing together complex clues to solve crimes. Still another might be a skilled negotiator, able to broker peaceful resolutions in high-stakes situations. Each individual's strengths contribute to the effectiveness of the entire team (1 Corinthians 12:15-16). It's not just about individual achievements but the synergistic power of different skills working together. The same is true in every aspect of community service.

This process of self-discovery is ongoing; it's a journey of continuous learning and refinement. Your gifts and talents might evolve and mature over time, as your experiences shape and mold your abilities. Embrace the process of self-reflection, and trust that God is guiding you towards your unique purpose.

Think about the specific skills that are valuable in the fields of emergency response and community service. Do you possess strong communication skills? Are you a natural leader, able to inspire and motivate others? Do you have a talent for organization or problem-solving? Are you empathetic, able to connect with people on a deep emotional level? Do you possess patience, perseverance, and the ability to remain calm under pressure? These are all valuable attributes in both fields, and the ability to identify and utilize them is key.

Consider the specific examples in your own life. Maybe you've always been drawn to helping others. Perhaps you've volunteered at a local shelter, tutored children, or helped with community cleanup projects. These actions might seem small, but they reveal your underlying motivations, indicating what truly matters to you, what resonates with your soul. Those are clear signals of your divinely appointed calling.

Perhaps you have excelled academically, demonstrating a sharp mind and a passion for learning. This intellectual capacity can be channeled into countless avenues of service, from teaching underprivileged children to conducting crucial research for non-profits. Or perhaps you are a skilled craft person, with a talent for building or repairing things. Your skills might be invaluable in providing aid to those in need of repair services or helping construct shelters for the homeless. Don't underestimate the power of your practical skills; they are gifts that can directly impact those around you.

Even seemingly mundane skills can be transformed into powerful instruments of service. Are you an excellent listener? Your ability to actively listen and empathize can provide solace and support to those who are struggling. Are you a good organizer? Your organizational skills can help streamline operations at a local charity or improve the efficiency of community-based initiatives. These seemingly simple skills, when combined with a passionate heart, can become significant forces for good.

Finally, remember that identifying your gifts is only the first step. The next crucial step is to take action, to put your talents to work in service to God and your community. Don't be afraid to step outside of your comfort zone and try new things. Embrace challenges, learn from your mistakes, and never stop seeking opportunities to grow and develop your gifts. The world is waiting

for your unique contribution. Your talents are not merely personal assets; they are sacred gifts entrusted to you for a divine purpose. Embracing your calling is embracing the beautiful symphony of your unique strengths, playing your part in God's orchestra of service.

Finding Your Place— Opportunities for Service

I have briefly written about the instruments within you, the gifts God has so graciously bestowed upon each and every one of us. We have plumbed the depths of self-assessment, recognizing our strengths, acknowledging our weaknesses, and understanding that the journey of faith is not about perfection but about persistent, faithful striving. Now, the question becomes: how do we put these instruments to use? How do we translate our talents, our passions, our unique blend of skills and desires, into tangible acts of service?

The answer lies in actively seeking opportunities to serve. It's not a passive waiting game; it's a proactive engagement with the world around us, a conscious decision to step out of our comfort zones and into the waiting arms of God's purpose. This isn't about grand gestures or heroic acts; often, the most profound impact comes from the smallest, most consistent deeds of love.

Let's explore some avenues, some pathways that will lead you to your place of service. Think of these not as limitations, but as launching pads, springboards to propel you into a life of purposeful action.

First, consider the immediate needs of your local community. Is there a food bank struggling to keep shelves stocked? Perhaps a homeless shelter needing extra hands to serve meals or assist with administrative tasks. These are tangible, immediate needs that can be met with direct action. The experience of personally handing a warm meal to a hungry person, of offering a comforting word to someone experiencing hardship, is a profoundly spiritual act.

It's a humbling reminder of our shared humanity and the power of simple kindness. Many churches have established outreach programs. Volunteer at your place of worship. Even offering a few hours a week to help with administrative tasks, cleaning, or children's programs can make a significant difference. Your talents, honed in your professional life, might be perfect for organizing a fundraiser, updating a website, or even offering legal advice to those in need. Remember, the skills you have developed aren't just for your personal gain; they are tools with which God has entrusted you to build His kingdom here on earth. Think beyond the immediate confines of your religious community. Local hospitals, senior centers, and schools are often in need of volunteers. Hospitals may need volunteers to assist patients and their families, offer companionship, or run errands. Senior centers may require volunteers to help with activities, transportation, or companionship for lonely elderly individuals. Schools often need assistance with tutoring, mentoring, or helping with special events. Each of these places offers a unique opportunity to extend love and support, to make a tangible difference in the lives of others.

Consider environmental initiatives. Our planet is crying out for our help, for our commitment to preserving its beauty and ensuring its sustainability. From participating in local clean-up drives to joining environmental organizations, there are countless ways to make a positive impact. Planting trees, raising awareness about conservation, and advocating for sustainable practices are all meaningful ways to demonstrate your commitment to stewardship of creation. Remember, God entrusted us with this beautiful world, and caring for it is an act of worship.

For those with a passion for justice, consider volunteering with organizations that fight for human rights, advocate for social justice, or provide legal services to the underserved. Perhaps your background in law enforcement or community service has equipped you with skills uniquely suited to these endeavors. Your experience, your insight, your empathy can be invaluable assets in the fight for a more equitable and just world. Remember, justice is a fundamental pillar of faith, and working to create a fairer society is a direct reflection of your devotion.

Think also about mentoring. This is a powerful way to make a lasting impact on the lives of young people. Mentoring doesn't require grand gestures or formal training; it simply requires a willingness to invest your time and energy in a young person's life, offering guidance, support, and encouragement. Many schools and community organizations have mentoring programs that connect volunteers with young people in need. Sharing your life experiences, offering wisdom gained through your own trials and triumphs, can be a profoundly transformative experience for both the mentor and the mentee.

Consider your professional skills. Are you a skilled writer? Offer to write grants for non-profits or create compelling content for their websites. Are you a skilled accountant or financial planner? Offer your expertise to help organizations manage their finances. Are you a talented musician or artist? Share your gifts through performances or workshops. Even seemingly small skills can be invaluable assets to community organizations. The point is to take what God has given you and utilize it for the good of others.

Don't underestimate the power of simply being present. Sometimes, the greatest act of service is simply listening— offering a compassionate ear to someone who needs to share their burdens, offering a presence that communicates love and acceptance. A simple act of kindness, a listening ear, a helping hand—these small gestures, repeated consistently, can have a ripple effect, extending far beyond the immediate recipient.

The opportunities are vast and varied, limited only by your imagination and your willingness to embrace the call. Remember, this is not just about ticking boxes or fulfilling obligations; it's about discovering your place within God's grand plan, about understanding your unique role in the tapestry of service. It's about finding joy in giving, finding fulfillment in serving others, and discovering the profound satisfaction of living a life of purpose.

Let me offer a practical framework for this search:

1. **Self-Reflection:** Take time for quiet contemplation. Pray for guidance. Ask God to reveal the areas where your talents and passions can best serve His purposes. Consider journaling, meditation, or spending time in nature to facilitate this reflection.

2. **Research:** Explore the various organizations and initiatives in your community. Look at their websites, attend their events, and talk to people who are involved. Find out what their needs are and how your skills could be a fit.

3. **Networking:** Talk to friends, family, and colleagues. Let them know you're looking for opportunities to serve and ask if they know of any organizations or initiatives that could be a good fit.

4. **Trial and Error:** Don't be afraid to try different things. You may find that some opportunities aren't the right fit for you, and that's okay. The important thing is to keep searching and to remain open to new possibilities.

5. **Persistence:** Finding your place of service may take time. Don't get discouraged if you don't find the perfect opportunity

immediately. Keep seeking, keep praying, and keep trusting in God's guidance.

Remember, the journey of faith is not a solitary one. We are called to walk alongside one another, to support and encourage each other, and to work together to build God's kingdom here on Earth. So, brothers and sisters, let us go forth and answer the call. Let us embrace the opportunities to serve and let us become instruments of God's love in the world. Let us be the hands and feet of Jesus, extending His grace and mercy to all those in need. Let our lives be a testament to the transformative power of faith in action.

Overcoming Barriers and Obstacles

We have laid the groundwork, and identified the gifts within, the unique talents God has bestowed upon each of us. We have acknowledged our strengths and weaknesses, understanding that the journey is one of continuous growth, not of flawless perfection. But the path to fulfilling our calling isn't always smooth. Obstacles, like jagged rocks in a rushing water, can threaten to divert us from our course. Let's address some of these common barriers, these impediments that might whisper doubts in our ears and try to hold us back from answering God's call.

The first, and perhaps most frequently cited, obstacle is the tyranny of time. "I don't have enough time," we cry, overwhelmed by the demands of work, family, and the relentless pressures of modern life. This is a legitimate concern, and it's not a sign of weakness to acknowledge the limitations of our schedules. But I ask you to consider the immeasurable value of even a small contribution of time. Does God require grand gestures, sweeping pronouncements of service? No. He sees the widow's mite, the humble act of kindness performed in quiet anonymity.

Think of it this way: Can you spare fifteen minutes a week? Could you dedicate an hour a month? Perhaps you can commit to a single day each quarter. These seemingly insignificant moments, when added together, can accumulate into a powerful and meaningful impact. Consider volunteering at a local soup kitchen for an hour, offering to help a neighbor with yard work, mentoring a child, or simply listening to a friend in need. These are not massive undertakings, but they are acts of service, born from love and fueled by faith. Even small acts can build a bridge towards a larger commitment over time.

Another significant barrier is fear. Fear of failure, fear of judgment, fear of the unknown—these insidious emotions can paralyze us, preventing us from stepping forward and embracing our callings. Fear whispers lies, telling us we're not good enough, not qualified enough, not worthy enough. Remember God doesn't always call the qualified; but He always qualifies the called.

He equips, guides, and strengthens us. Your perceived inadequacies are not barriers to God's work; they are opportunities for His grace to shine even brighter.

Remember the story of Gideon in Judges 6:11-24? He was initially terrified at the prospect of leading the Israelites to victory. He felt utterly inadequate, but God reassured him, proving His strength through miraculous signs. God doesn't call the perfect; He perfects the called. Embrace your imperfections, knowing that your vulnerabilities are not weaknesses but pathways to a deeper connection with God and a more profound expression of His love. The journey is about faith, not perfection. Self-doubt, a close cousin to fear, can be equally debilitating. It's that insidious voice in our heads that questions our abilities, our worthiness, our capacity to make a difference. We might minimize our talents, believing our contributions are insignificant. This is a deceptive

voice; don't listen to it. Your unique skills and passions, however seemingly small, are gifts from God, intended to be used for His glory. Every individual possesses a unique perspective, a unique set of experiences, and a unique set of talents that contribute to the larger tapestry of God's work.

Don't allow self-doubt to steal your joy, your purpose, your potential. Instead, focus on your strengths, celebrate your accomplishments, and trust in God's unwavering support. Seek out mentors, confidants, and fellow believers who can offer encouragement and affirmation. Surround yourself with a supportive community that will lift you up and help you overcome the insidious whispers of self-doubt. Another common hurdle is the perceived lack of opportunity. "Where do I even begin?" many might ask. "There are so many needs, so many causes, that I feel overwhelmed and paralyzed by all the options." This feeling is understandable, but it shouldn't prevent us from taking action. Begin with what's close at hand. Look around your community, your family, your circle of friends. Who needs help? Where can you make a difference?

It could be as simple as volunteering at your local church, tutoring underprivileged children, visiting the sick, or donating to a worthy cause. The possibilities are endless, and the opportunities are often closer than we realize. Don't wait for some grand, dramatic opportunity; God often speaks to us in quiet moments, through subtle nudges and opportunities for everyday acts of kindness. Be open to those opportunities. Listen to the promptings of the Holy Spirit and let Him guide you toward the specific path of service He has intended for you.

Finally, let's address the issue of discouragement. The path to fulfilling your calling is not always easy. You will encounter setbacks, disappointments, and moments when you question whether you're making any real difference. This is part of the journey, and it's crucial to remember that persistence is key. Don't allow temporary setbacks to derail your purpose.

Celebrate small victories, learn from your mistakes, and persevere in faith. Remember that God is with you every step of the way. His grace is sufficient, and His strength is made perfect in our weakness (2 Corinthians 12:9).

The path to answering God's call is not a race; it's a marathon. It requires patience, perseverance, and an unwavering trust in His plan for your life. Remember that we are called to work together, to support and encourage one another. Don't be afraid to ask for help, seek guidance, and lean on the strength of your community. We are all on this journey together, and we are all called to contribute to the building of God's kingdom on Earth. Embrace the challenges, overcome the obstacles, and never underestimate the power of your unique gifts and talents.

Let your life be a testament to the transformative power of faith in action, a beacon of hope shining brightly in this world, a living testament to the love and grace of our Lord. Remember even the smallest act of service, performed with love and faith, can make a profound difference in the lives of others and in the world around us. Let us go forth with unwavering faith and courageous hearts to answer the call.

Celebrating Successes—Acknowledging and Honoring Contributions

We have talked about the hurdles, the trials, the moments of doubt that can assail us on our journey to answering God's call. But let's now shift our focus. Let's talk about victory. Let's talk about celebrating the triumphs, big and small, that mark our progress along this path of service. Because the work we do in His name, the service we offer to our communities, deserves not only our tireless effort, but also our heartfelt recognition and celebration.

Too often, we get caught up in the relentless pursuit of our goals, our focus laser-beamed on the next task, the next challenge. We push forward, driven by faith and a desire to serve, but we forget to pause, to reflect, to acknowledge the ground we have already covered. We forget to celebrate the victories, both individual and collective, that are the steppingstones to even greater achievements. This isn't about self-congratulation, but about recognizing the power of positive reinforcement, the crucial role of appreciation in fueling our continued commitment to serving others.

Think about it. A police officer, after a long night spent apprehending criminals, bringing justice to those who desperately need it, often returns to a quiet station, a quiet acknowledgement. The community they protect might never know the intricacies of their work, the bravery, the cunning, the dedication it takes. Yet, the simple act of a superior officer expressing gratitude, a fellow officer offering a word of encouragement, can make all the difference. It replenishes the spirit and renews the commitment. It reminds officers that their efforts are seen, valued, and appreciated.

This principle transcends the realm of law enforcement. Consider the tireless volunteers at a homeless shelter, the dedicated teachers in underfunded schools, the compassionate nurses working long shifts in understaffed hospitals. These individuals, these unsung heroes, often work tirelessly, pouring their hearts and souls into their service, receiving little in the way of tangible reward. Yet, the simple act of acknowledging their commitment, dedication, and selflessness, can be a powerful source of encouragement, a vital catalyst for continued service.

Celebrating successes doesn't require grand gestures or lavish celebrations. Sometimes, the most profound expressions of gratitude are the simplest. A heartfelt thank you note, a personal word of appreciation, a small token of recognition—these seemingly insignificant acts can have a tremendous impact on the morale and motivation of individuals and organizations dedicated to community service.

Think about the impact of a simple "thank you" on a volunteer at a soup kitchen. The repetitive nature of their task, serving meal after meal to the less fortunate, can lead to burnout if their selfless efforts are never recognized. A sincere "thank you" for their time, compassion, and dedication can reignite their passion, reminding them of the profound impact they're having on the lives of those they serve.

Similarly, consider the effect of a public acknowledgment on a community organization. A small article in the local newspaper highlighting their achievements, a commendation from a local official, or a simple ceremony recognizing their contributions— these actions can not only boost the morale of the organization's members but also inspire others to join their cause. They demonstrate that their hard work is valued, that their efforts are making a difference, and that their contributions are appreciated.

This is not merely about boosting morale; it's about fostering a culture of appreciation, a culture where every act of service, no matter how small, is recognized and celebrated. This culture of appreciation creates a ripple effect, inspiring others to participate, contribute, and join in the pursuit of a better world. It encourages a sense of camaraderie and shared purpose, strengthening the bonds between individuals and organizations working towards a common goal.

Furthermore, celebrating successes fosters a culture of learning and continuous improvement. By taking the time to reflect on past achievements, we can identify what worked well, what challenges we overcame, and what lessons we learned. This process of reflection allows us to improve our strategies, refine our techniques, and ultimately become more effective in our service to others. It allows us to build upon our successes, laying a solid foundation for even greater achievements in the future.

Now, I understand that some might argue that celebrating successes is a distraction from the important work at hand. They might say that our focus should remain solely on serving others rather than acknowledging our own accomplishments. But I believe that these two aspects are not mutually exclusive. In fact, they are inextricably linked. Celebrating our successes doesn't diminish our commitment to service; rather, it fuels it. It renews our energy, strengthens our resolve, and inspires us to continue serving with renewed vigor and passion. Consider the practical application. In a community center, for instance, a simple monthly meeting to highlight the successes of the month—volunteers who consistently go above and beyond, donations that have made a real difference, programs that have achieved significant results—can create a powerful sense of shared accomplishment and collective pride. This monthly celebration can not only boost morale but also foster a sense of belonging and camaraderie among the volunteers and staff.

In a faith-based organization, this celebration might take the form of a service acknowledging the contributions of various ministries. Highlighting the successes of the youth ministry, the outreach program, or the food bank, can instill a sense of pride and unity amongst the congregation, strengthening their commitment to serving the community. It reminds them of the collective power of their faith in action.

Let's think about how we can apply this in our own lives. Are we taking the time to acknowledge the achievements of our fellow servants? Are we expressing gratitude for their tireless efforts? Are we creating a culture of appreciation within our communities, our organizations, and our families?

If not, let us begin today. Let us make a conscious effort to celebrate the successes, big and small, that mark our progress along this path of service.

The Ongoing Journey of Service— Continuous Growth and Development

We have celebrated the victories, acknowledged the grace, and felt the warmth of community in our shared journey of service. But the path of faith, the path of service, is not a sprint; it's a marathon, a lifelong commitment to growing in grace, wisdom, and the unwavering pursuit of God's will. This isn't about reaching a destination; it's about embracing the journey itself—a journey of continuous growth and development. The mighty oak, a symbol of strength and resilience doesn't spring forth fully formed; it begins as a tiny sapling, vulnerable to the elements, yet possessing within it the potential for majestic growth. The oak endures harsh winters, scorching summers, and relentless storms. Yet, through it all, it continues to grow, its roots deepening, its branches reaching for the heavens. This, my friends, is a parable for our lives of service.

Our service, our commitment to our communities, is much like that young oak. It requires nurturing, it requires tending, and it demands a constant commitment to growth. We must never become complacent, never assume that we have reached our full potential. The ongoing journey of service necessitates a commitment to lifelong learning. This means actively seeking out opportunities for personal and professional development.

It means embracing challenges and setbacks not as failures, but as opportunities for growth and refinement. It means surrounding

ourselves with mentors, fellow servants, and individuals who challenge and inspire us to become better versions of ourselves. Another aspect to consider about the parable of the talents is those who diligently used their talents were rewarded not for their initial abilities, but for their commitment to growth and expansion.

How do we cultivate this continuous growth? First, through consistent self-reflection. We must regularly examine our motivations, our methods, and the impact we are making on the lives of others. Are we truly serving God's purpose? Are we approaching our tasks with humility, compassion, and a genuine desire to uplift those around us? Honest self-assessment is crucial. It allows us to identify areas where we excel and areas where we need improvement. It encourages us to hone our skills, refine our approach, and become more effective servants of the Lord.

Second, seek out diverse learning experiences. Don't limit yourselves to what you already know. Step outside of your comfort zones and engage in experiences that stretch your abilities and expand your horizons. Perhaps you are called to serve the homeless population but have never worked directly with people experiencing poverty. Embrace the challenge. Learn about the issues they face, the struggles they overcome, and the dignity they deserve. Learn from their stories, their resilience, and their unwavering faith.

This might involve taking additional training courses, attending workshops and seminars, or pursuing further education. It could also mean engaging in cross-cultural service opportunities. The world is vast and diverse, and there are countless ways to serve. By exposing ourselves to new cultures, new perspectives, and new challenges, we broaden our understanding of God's creation and deepen our capacity for empathy and compassion.

Third, embrace mentorship and peer learning. We are not alone on this journey. Surround yourself with individuals who can guide, encourage, and support you. Seek out mentors who have experience in the field you are serving, individuals who have successfully navigated the challenges and triumphs of a life dedicated to service. Learn from their successes and their mistakes. Their wisdom and guidance will prove invaluable as we navigate our own path.

Equally important is the power of peer learning. Engage with others who share your passion for service. Share your experiences, your challenges, and your triumphs. Learn from their perspectives and share your wisdom in return. A strong support network can sustain you through difficult times, bolster your spirit during moments of doubt, and inspire you to continue your commitment to service.

Fourth, remember the importance of community. Our work in the Lord's name is not a solitary endeavor; it is a collaborative effort. We are part of a vast and interconnected body of believers, working together to build God's kingdom on earth. Engage with your local church, volunteer organizations, and community initiatives. Find ways to collaborate with others, leveraging your collective strengths to create a greater impact. Remember the power of prayer and spiritual fellowship. Seek solace and strength through shared worship and fellowship.

Fifth, celebrate your successes. As we have discussed, we must acknowledge our triumphs, big and small. Celebrating achievements encourages us to persevere. It reminds us of the progress we have made and inspires us to continue our journey of service. Sharing our stories of success can inspire others to answer God's call and to embark on their own journeys of service.

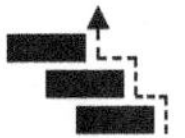

Sixth, never underestimate the power of continuous learning. Our world is constantly evolving, and so too must our approaches to service. New challenges arise, new needs emerge, and we must adapt and grow to meet them effectively. Stay abreast of current events, research the latest techniques and methodologies, and remain open to new ideas and approaches. Embrace innovation and explore new ways of serving others.

Seventh, remember the ultimate goal: to glorify God through your service. Let your actions be a testament to your faith, a reflection of your love for God and your fellow human beings. Let your service be an act of worship, a selfless offering to the One who has given you so much.

The ongoing journey of service is not a destination; it is a pilgrimage of faith, a lifelong commitment to growth and development, and a testament to the power of love and compassion. Embrace the challenges, celebrate the victories, and always strive to become a better servant of our Lord.

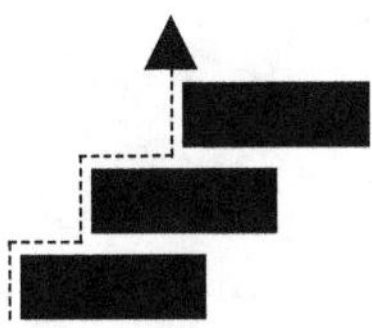

THE GREATEST STEP

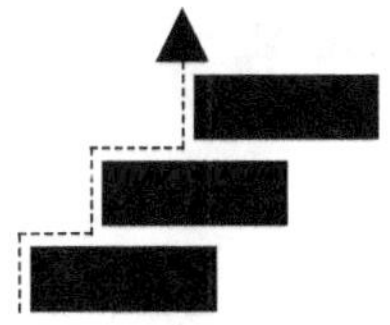

THE STEP OF SALVATION

Accepting Jesus Christ as your personal savior is the wisest and best decision you can make. This decision results in what we call salvation. Salvation is being saved from one's sins. Sin is anything that is contrary to God's commands and standard for one's life. I heard it explained as a person falling short of the mark. This mark is set by God and has to do with good and evil. Think of a dart game. The preferred target is the bull's-eye or the 100. Sin would be falling short of that bull's-eye.

We need to know three important things about a person's condition prior to salvation. These things are:

1. Everyone is a sinner. We are not sinners because we sin; we sin because we are sinners by nature. We were born with this nature because of the sin of the first couple, Adam and Eve.

2. We cannot save ourselves. No matter what we do, we cannot make out standing right with God. We are powerless to remove sin or control the sin nature—the tendency to want to sin.

3. Only Jesus Christ has the power to save us from these conditions—sin and the sin nature.

The Bible declares that "all have sinned" (Romans 3:23) and that the result of sin is death (Romans 6:23). This death is not physical, but spiritual death. Death is not non-existence, rather it is separation. Sin separates us spiritually from God.

A relationship with God is not possible where sin is not canceled out, sin cannot be not canceled out by a person's good deeds or thoughts. We can have our sin canceled out by Jesus Christ alone. Jesus Christ made a way for our sins to be canceled. When He died on the cross, He took our place and paid sin's penalty and suffered our punishment. For the results of His act to be yours, you must believe that Jesus died on the cross to pay for your sin and ask God the Father to forgive you for your sins.

When you do this, God the Father will accept you for Jesus' sake. Your sins will then be forgiven, and Jesus will become your personal savior. You will be alive spiritually, connected to God, and have a new nature with all its God-designed opportunities. If you are ready for this step, you can change your life today by simply praying this prayer out loud before the Lord!

Dear Heavenly Father,

I come to you in the name of Your Son, Jesus. Your Word says that "Whoever calls on God in the Name of the Lord will be saved, and "If I will confess with my mouth the Lord Jesus and will believe in my heart that God has raised Jesus from the dead, I will be saved" (Read Acts 2:21 & Romans 10:9-10). I believe Your Word and confess Jesus as the Lord of my life. I believe that You raised Your Son Jesus from the dead and He is now seated with You in heaven and, one day, will return to earth for those who are saved. Come into my heart and save me now from my sins and from eternal death which would separate me from You forever. I want to live my life for You. Change me now. (Read John 3:5–7, 16, 17 & Romans 8:9–11.) Amen.

If you have just taken this step, or have questions, please contact a chaplain, pastor, or someone that you know to be a Christian so that they can share with you how you can grow in your walk with God.

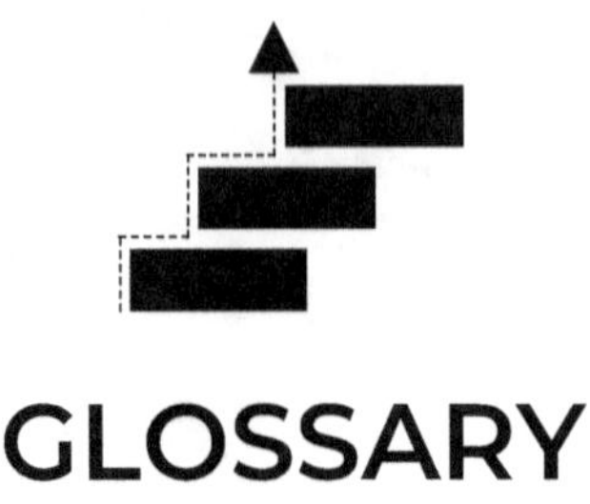

GLOSSARY

This glossary defines key terms used throughout the book:

Active Listening: A communication technique focused on fully understanding the speaker's message, both verbally and nonverbally.

Compassion: Empathy in action; a deep feeling of sympathy and concern for others, coupled with a desire to help.

Compliance: Adherence to rules, regulations, and established protocols; teamwork and collaboration.

Courage: The ability to act despite fear or adversity; facing challenges with bravery and resolve.

First Responder: Individuals who are among the first to arrive at the scene of an emergency.

Ministry of Presence: Providing support and comfort simply by being present and offering empathy and understanding.

Self-Deployment: Acting independently without proper authorization or coordination; dangerous and often ineffective.

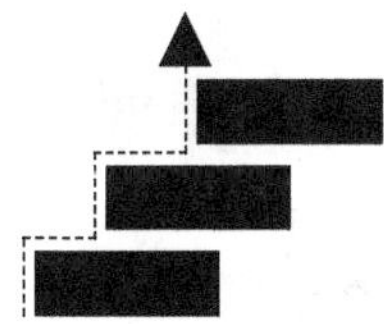

STEPS TO SUCCESS
PODCAST

Empowering individuals to unlock their full potential, the show offers a roadmap for achieving personal and ministry success, rooted in biblical principles and practical advice.

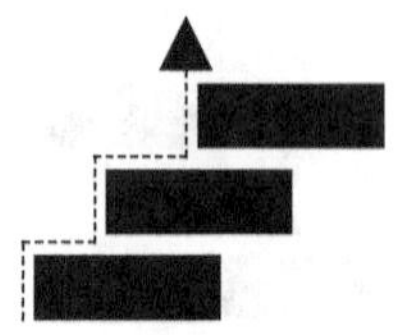

ABOUT THE AUTHOR

Jonathan, an Assemblies of God USA Commissioned Emergency Services Chaplain with Advanced Ecclesiastical Endorsement with The Assemblies of God Commission on Chaplains, is the Lead Pastor of Glad Tidings Tabernacle, Caribbean Regional Commander for Frontline Chaplains International, and a Chaplain Coordinator with The Billy Graham RRT.

He has dedicated his life to serving God and his community, bringing together his experiences with his deep-rooted faith. He is passionate about equipping first responders and chaplains with the spiritual and practical tools they need to thrive in their demanding roles.

In acknowledgment of his significant contributions in the United States as a chaplain and first responder, Jonathan received the U.S. President's Lifetime Achievement Award for Community Service and Volunteerism in 2023. Jonathan has a background in non-fiction writing and is committed to sharing this message of courage, compassion, and compliance with a wider audience. He currently resides in Key West, Florida, with his family.

Website: stepstosuccess.us

Email: info@stepstosuccess.us